Collins

frontline history

United States

1918 – 1941

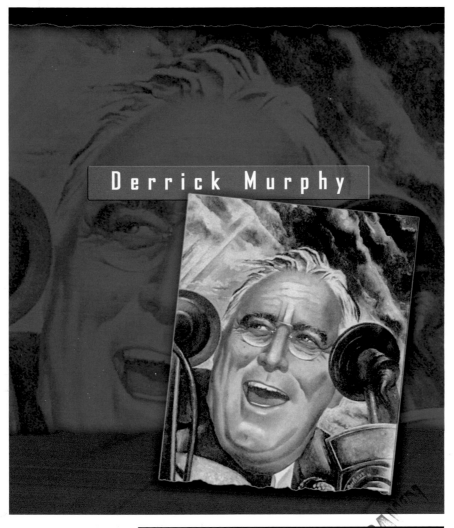

Derrick Murphy

SERIES EDITOR: DERRICK MURPHY

Published by Collins Educational
An imprint of HarperCollins*Publishers* Ltd
77–85 Fulham Palace Road
Hammersmith
London
W6 8JB

www.**Collins**Education.com
On-line support for schools and colleges

© HarperCollins*Publishers* Ltd 2003
First published 2003

ISBN 0 00 715119 5

Derrick Murphy asserts his moral right to be identified as the author of this work.

British Library Cataloguing in Publication Data.
A catalogue record for this publication is available from the British Library.

Edited by Will Chuter
Design by Sally Boothroyd
Cover design by BarkerHilsdon
Picture research by Celia Dearing
Artwork by Richard Morris
Production by Katie Morris
Printed and bound by Printing Express Ltd, Hong Kong
Index compiled by Julie Rimington

Contents

Using your factual knowledge of the USA between 1918 and 1941 effectively is very important to success at GCSE Modern World History. This book is designed to provide the essential information. It contains:

- The important questions asked at GCSE
- Detailed information about key historical events and characters
- Written and visual sources
- Differing historical interpretations about the period you are studying

This Study Skills section is designed to help you do your best at GCSE Modern World History. Many of the skills are developments from what you covered in Key Stage 3 History:

- How to explain and use written sources
- How to evaluate cartoons, posters, photographs, maps and graphs
- How to develop extended writing

When you are studying the individual topics in this book make sure that you refer back to these pages for guidance.

HOW TO EXPLAIN AND USE WRITTEN SOURCES

You may have learnt at Key Stage 3 that there are two types of source: primary and secondary. Primary sources are either produced at the time of the event or produced after the event by a witness of the event. Secondary sources are those written after the event by someone who did not witness the event. Although knowing whether a source is primary or secondary is important, it is more important to explain whether it is **useful** or **reliable**.

What does a source show?
Sometimes you are asked to explain what a source reveals about a particular subject. **Remember: always look at the precise wording of a question.** The question may only ask you to explain certain parts of the source.

EXAMPLE 1 – look at the biography of Wilson, p10

Question What does this source reveal about Woodrow Wilson and the First World War?
In your answer, you need to identify that Wilson tried to keep the USA out of the war before 1917. He even promised he would do this in the 1916 presidential election campaign. However, you should avoid simply describing the information in the source. Several sections are not relevant for this question. These include the information that Wilson was a university lecturer, had been Governor of New Jersey before he became President, and that he was an invalid from October 1919.

How reliable is a source?
A reliable source is one that contains an accurate or objective view of a past event. Because different people see past events from different viewpoints, it is difficult for any source to be completely reliable. **Be careful: both primary sources and secondary sources may be unreliable.**

What makes a source unreliable?
A source may be unreliable because it contains **bias**. This means that the person producing the source may wish to look at a past event from a particular viewpoint. The person might have a **motive** for producing the source in a particular way.

EXAMPLE 2 – look at Source 2, p36

Question How reliable is this source as evidence of why the USA suffered from economic depression after October 1929?
Ask yourself these questions:

- *Did the person writing the source have a motive for not telling the truth?*
Yes. President Hoover was head of the US government in 1930. He was seen by many Americans as responsible for the economic depression. Hoover, in the source, is trying to pass the blame for the economic depression on to factors outside the USA and therefore out of his control. He is trying to divert the blame from himself.

- *Does the source contain **objective** or **subjective** information?*
Objective information means factual information. Subjective information means someone's opinion.
If a source contains a lot of subjective information, it is likely to be **biased**. This source contains both objective and subjective information.
Objective information: "Overproduction of certain goods abroad… political trouble in Asia… revolutions in South America".
Subjective information: "Worldwide causes… have all contributed to… the Depression".

Even though a source may contain a lot of facts (objective information) it may still be unreliable. **You will need to test the information against your own knowledge or other sources.**

Much of the information that Hoover mentions is true. However, he does not mention causes of the economic depression from within the USA, in particular those for which he can be blamed personally. These include: government policy; domestic overproduction and under-consumption; speculation in shares on the stock market; unequal distribution of wealth within the USA during the 1920s.

How useful is a source?

To answer this question correctly you need to think about exactly whom it's useful to. Usually this appears in the question: 'How useful is this source to a historian writing about…?'

To decide how useful a source might be you need to look at its strengths, then list them. Then decide what the source's limitations are – what it doesn't mention – then list them. Once you have done this, look at your lists. Does the source contain more strengths than weaknesses? If so, you could say that the source is quite useful.

EXAMPLE 3 – look at Source 2, p39

Question How useful is this source as evidence of opinion about the New York Stock Market in October 1929?

List of strengths
• It is from an article in a New York newspaper.
• The article was written in October 1929.
• It shows the opinion of a financial journalist, someone knowledgeable about the stock market.

List of limitations
• It only shows the opinion of one person – a New York financial journalist – not the opinion of anyone else, from anywhere else in the USA.
• The opinion is only based on events in October 1929 up to October 22. It does not cover the last nine days of October, which included Black Thursday (October 24) and Black Tuesday (October 28). On these days, share prices fell dramatically. This was the Wall Street Crash. Following this, share prices did not "gain momentum", but stayed very low until 1932. Opinion about the New York stock market might have been very different after the Wall Street Crash.

The source contains only a limited amount of information. You need to **test this information against your own knowledge to decide how useful it is**.

HOW TO EVALUATE VISUAL SOURCES

Cartoons, photographs, posters, graphs, and maps are all different types of visual sources. **As with written sources, you also need to test the usefulness and reliability of visual sources.**

Cartoons

Cartoons are usually produced to convey a political **message**. Cartoons are used because they can give an immediate, visual message in a way that a written source cannot.

EXAMPLE 4 – look at Source 2, p45

This cartoon was produced at the time of FD Roosevelt's inauguration as President. It shows FDR throwing out former President Hoover's policies. Hoover is shown walking away on the right of the cartoon. The cartoonist is a supporter of FDR. So he has a **motive** for showing FDR and Hoover is this way.

The cartoon is making a political point. It shows FDR as an active person, personally getting rid of Hoover's policies. FDR is smiling, suggesting that he is enjoying ending Hoover's policies and introducing his own. FDR is active and energetic. This suggests he is the right man for the job of getting the USA out of economic depression.

However, using your own knowledge of the period you will know that FDR suffered the effects of polio. In fact, in March 1933 FDR could only stand with the assistance of steel braces on his legs and the support of another person.

You will also know that when Hoover campaigned for the presidency in 1928, he claimed that the Republicans would provide every American with enough food ('chicken in every pot'), and luxuries ('car in every garage'). Clearly, by March 1933 these things had not materialised for every American. The cartoon reflects that.

Now look at the other 11 cartoons in the book. Use the points above to evaluate the message of these cartoons.

Photographs

'The camera never lies!' This is a commonly used phrase that is not necessarily true. Sometimes a picture does not tell the whole story. Therefore you need to **test** the photograph by providing **corroborative** evidence. This means using your own knowledge or referring to other sources.

EXAMPLE 5 – look at Source 1, p58

Question Does this photograph prove that African-Americans experienced racial discrimination in the USA in the 1930s?
This photograph shows a white and an African-American using separate drinking fountains in the Old South in the 1930s. From your own knowledge you can note that, in the states of the Old South, African-Americans were forced to live segregated lives. They had to attend separate schools from whites, live in different areas from whites, and, in some cases, face violent acts by whites.

Now look at Source 3 on page 17. This shows a lynching of two African-Americans in Indiana. This suggests that African-Americans faced violent attacks and discrimination even outside the Old South.

Not every African-American suffered badly at the time. Louis Armstrong (see p33) was an African-American musician. In the 1920s and 1930s he became one of the most popular entertainers both for whites and African-Americans in Europe, as well as the USA.

So, the first photograph does not prove that African-Americans experienced racial discrimination in the USA in the 1930s – it only proves that it was a problem in the Old South. You need to look at other sources and your own knowledge to be able to answer the question fully.

Posters
Posters are usually produced for a particular reason. They tend to serve the purposes of the person who has paid for them to be made. These people have **motives** for presenting the poster in a particular way.

EXAMPLE 6 – look at Source 1, p10

Question How does this poster encourage people to join the US Navy during the First World War?
This poster has been produced by the US government. Their motive is to get as many men as possible to join the navy. They use the image of women and children drowning at sea to highlight the German policy of unrestricted U-boat warfare. The passenger ship Lusitania is shown sinking in the background. It was torpedoed in 1915. This was a major reason for the USA's entrance into the First World War. It tries to appeal to emotions. Men would be attracted to joining the navy in order to protect US women and children and stop this kind of thing happening.

EXAMPLE 7 – look at Source 4, p27

Question Does this poster fully explain why national prohibition was introduced in the USA in 1920?
This poster was produced by the Strengthen America Campaign. This organisation (and others, like the Anti-Saloon League) wanted to ban the manufacture, sale and consumption of alcoholic drinks across the USA. It tries to give certain reasons – especially moral reasons – to ban alcohol. It suggests that drinking alcohol damages the family, especially the upbringing of young children. But this only presents one side of the argument for introducing prohibition. Again, you need to look at corroborative evidence for the other sides (see p27). Having understood this, you should be more able to judge whether the poster fully explains why prohibition was introduced.

Graphs, maps and statistical data
Graphs, maps and statistical data are sometimes used to help students understand information more easily than providing a written source.

EXAMPLE 8 – look at Source 1, p38

This shows the dramatic change in share prices of major US companies following the Wall Street Crash of October 1929.

Statistical data gives you precise information. It also allows you to see change in a way a written source might not – it can show **trends**. But statistical data can have limitations. Although this source shows the actual changes in share price, it would be more useful if it also included the percentage change in price. Can you work out the percentage change in price of the shares in the source?

EXAMPLE 9 – look at the map, p49

Maps have a similar value. This shows clearly the area covered by the TVA and the location of dams in a way that a written source could not. It provides instant information to support FDR's scheme to produce electricity and control soil erosion in that area.

EXAMPLE 10 – look at Source 2, p40

Diagrams can be very useful in identifying **links** between different historical events. This diagram shows clearly the link between the fall in share prices on the Stock Market, the closure of factories and the rise in unemployment. It allows you to see the vicious circle effect on the US economy. You can see how this process developed to create the massive economic depression of the early 1930s.

HOW TO ANSWER EXTENDED WRITING QUESTIONS

These questions require a detailed factual answer. Knowing the information contained in this book is extremely important. To make sure that you use the information correctly you need to:

- **Make sure you answer the question on the paper.** It's a bad idea to write an answer for a question that is not on the paper just because you have prepared for it!

- **Make a short plan for your intended question.** This should show the order you want to set out the information in your answer. It will also help ensure you don't leave out important information whilst writing your answer.

- **Write in paragraphs.** Each paragraph should contain an important point you wish to make.

- **Remember important dates.** Or try to remember the sequence of events.

- **Use historical terms** (e.g. flapper, share speculation, WASP, normalcy) **correctly**.

- **Also use key words** (e.g. Congress, Supreme Court, Senate) **correctly**.

- **Understand the role of important individuals** (e.g. Presidents Wilson, Hoover and FD Roosevelt).

- **Make sure you spell historical words correctly.** You must also try to use good punctuation and grammar. Poor 'SPG' can cost you marks.

- **Try to make links between various paragraphs.** If you are asked either to explain or describe the causes of the economic depression in the USA, it is important to link causes. These could be:

> **Long Term Causes** The unequal distribution of wealth in the USA during the 1920s.
>
> **Short Term Causes** Overproduction and policies of the Republican governments of Harding, Coolidge and Hoover.
>
> **Immediate Cause** The Wall Street Crash of October 1929

- **Write a brief conclusion.** This could just be one sentence at the end. But it is essential because it contains your **judgement**. For example, in the question above, what would you regard as **the most important cause** of the Depression?

HOW THIS BOOK MATCHES THE EXAM SPECIFICATIONS

Chapters in this book	AQA History B, Paper 2, Option C	Edexcel History A, Paper 2, Section B	OCR History B, Depth Study C
1 POLITICS, PEOPLE AND PREJUDICES	9.5 Part 1: The growth of Isolation, 1919-1920; 9.5 Part 2: The Promised Land? The USA in the 1920s	N/A	Key Question 2: How far did US society change in the 1920s?
2 PROSPERITY, PROHIBITION AND POPULAR CULTURE	9.5 Part 2: The Promised Land? The USA in the 1920s	N/A	Key Question 1: How far did the US economy boom in the 1920s?; Key Question 2: How far did US society change in the 1920s?
3 THE GREAT DEPRESSION	9.5 Part 3: America in Depression, 1929-1933	B3: Depression and the New Deal: the USA, 1929-41	Key Question 3: What were the causes and consequences of the Wall Street Crash?
4 THE FIRST NEW DEAL	9.5 Part 4: Recovery from Depression, 1933-1941	B3: Depression and the New Deal: the USA, 1929-41	Key Question 4: How successful was the New Deal?
5 THE SECOND NEW DEAL	9.5 Part 4: Recovery from Depression, 1933-1941	B3: Depression and the New Deal: the USA, 1929-41	Key Question 4: How successful was the New Deal?

How was the USA governed from 1918 to 1941?

A FEDERAL STATE

The USA and Britain are both democracies. But the way these democracies work is very different. The USA is a federal state. This means that political power is divided between the federal (central) government and 48 individual state governments (see map). For instance, state governments are responsible for law and order. (If a person was convicted of murder, in the 1920s that person could face life imprisonment, be shot by firing squad, hanged, electrocuted or gassed with cyanide. It depended on which state you were in.) It wasn't until 1924 that a nationwide police force was created: the Federal Bureau of Investigation (FBI).

THE SEPARATION OF POWERS

To prevent the creation of a dictatorship, the Founding Fathers set up the separation of powers. This meant no person or institution had complete power of government or law-making. Power was divided at federal level between the President, the Congress (national parliament) and the Supreme Court. A president can sign international treaties. However, he needs the support of the Senate (Upper House of Congress) before it becomes law. The President can also choose all the senior members of government, but again he needs the 'advice and consent' of the Senate before they can be appointed.

> **Founding Fathers**
> the men who drew up the US Constitution in 1787. They included the first president George Washington

- - - - - - - - - - - - - - - **FACT FILE** - - - - - - - - - - - - - -

THE DIVISION OF POLITICAL POWER BETWEEN THE FEDERAL AND STATE GOVERNMENTS

Federal responsibilities
National defence
Conduct of foreign relations
Inter-state trade and commerce

State responsibilities
Education
Law and order
Welfare

A map showing the USA and its 48 states in 1918. Two extra states – Hawaii and Alaska – were added in 1959.

US Supreme Court
Contained nine judges chosen by the President with advice and consent of the Senate. Appointed for life. Had the power to interpret the US Constitution – it could declare actions by the President, Congress or States unconstitutional and therefore illegal.

Federal government
Head of government: the President (elected every four years).
President chooses members of the government with the advice and consent of the Senate.

Congress (the national parliament)
Two houses: the Senate and the House of Representatives

Senate
Contained 96 senators (two from each state, elected every six years).

House of Representatives
Contained 435 Congressmen, elected on basis of population. New York State had the largest number (46) and Wyoming the lowest (1).

State government
Each state had its own government, parliament and supreme court. The equivalent of the President in a state was the Governor.
Each state parliament had two houses – just like Congress – except Nebraska, which had only one. Governors and state parliaments could pass state laws.

HOW A FEDERAL LAW IS PASSED

The President or any member of Congress can propose a law. It has to be sent, simultaneously, to both houses of Congress: the Senate and House of Representatives. A Bill has to pass in both houses of Congress. Even then the President can veto it. Even with presidential support, the law might be declared unconstitutional by the Supreme Court.

ELECTIONS

From 1920 every American adult over 21 could vote in national, state and local elections. They could elect the President, Senators, Congressmen, the State Governor and Assemblymen. When choosing a President, each state voted separately. To win an election, a candidate had to win the majority of state electoral college votes. These were based on the number of Senators and Congressmen they had. New York State had 48 and Wyoming had just three. People who lived in Washington DC did not live in a State. They couldn't vote in presidential elections.

National elections took place every two years. As the President was elected every four years, the elections in the middle of his term were called mid-term elections. Even though a President was elected in November, he had to wait until March the following year to form the government. From 1933 onwards the time gap was reduced to late January.

POLITICAL PARTIES

US politics was dominated by two parties: the Democrats and the Republicans. The Democrats got support from whites in the Old South and from Irish, Jewish and Italian Americans. They also got support from trade unions. Republicans got support from businessmen and from most of the White, Anglo-Saxon Protestants (WASPs) outside the Old South. Up to 1933 African-Americans tended to vote Republican. From 1933 they switched to support the Democrats.

Questions

1. Explain the meaning of
   - a federal state
   - separation of powers
   - advice and consent
   - unconstitutional
2. Explain how a federal law was passed.
3. In what ways was the government of America different from the way modern Britain is governed? Draw a table to show the differences.

President Wilson – success or failure?

In April 1917 the USA had entered the First World War on the side of the Allied Powers, Britain, France, Russia and Italy. They were fighting Germany and Austria-Hungary. The US entry into the war helped bring an end to the stalemate between the two sides on the Western Front. The USA provided the Allies with food, munitions and another large army. Over 1.2 million Americans fought on the Western Front in 1918, and helped tip the balance in Allied favour. By November 11, 1918, the Germans had demanded either a ceasefire or an armistice and the war was over.

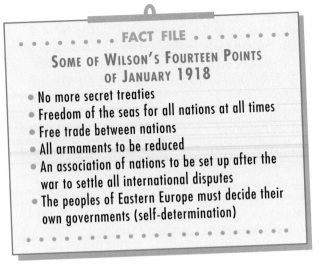

· · · · · · · · · · · FACT FILE · · · · · · · · · · ·
SOME OF WILSON'S FOURTEEN POINTS OF JANUARY 1918
- No more secret treaties
- Freedom of the seas for all nations at all times
- Free trade between nations
- All armaments to be reduced
- An association of nations to be set up after the war to settle all international disputes
- The peoples of Eastern Europe must decide their own governments (self-determination)

WHY WAS WILSON IMPORTANT DURING THE FIRST WORLD WAR?

President Wilson had brought the USA into the war because he was against the German policy of **unrestricted U-boat warfare**. In January 1918 Woodrow Wilson announced his 'Fourteen Points'. These were America's war aims. They were so popular that they became the unofficial war aims of the Allied side. When Germany agreed to an armistice in November 1918 they thought the peace treaty would be based on the Fourteen Points.

unrestricted U-boat warfare
German tactic of sinking any nation's ships, including US, to prevent supplies reaching Britain and France

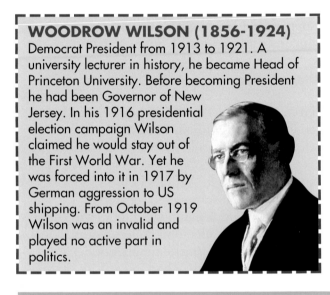

WOODROW WILSON (1856-1924)
Democrat President from 1913 to 1921. A university lecturer in history, he became Head of Princeton University. Before becoming President he had been Governor of New Jersey. In his 1916 presidential election campaign Wilson claimed he would stay out of the First World War. Yet he was forced into it in 1917 by German aggression to US shipping. From October 1919 Wilson was an invalid and played no active part in politics.

SHALL THIS CONTINUE?

JOIN THE NAVY

NAVY LEAGUE PITTSBURGH

ANCHOR BANK BUILDING

An American poster of 1917 encouraging US citizens to enlist in the navy.

HOW SUCCESSFUL WAS WILSON AT THE PARIS PEACE CONFERENCE?

When the war ended, a peace conference was held in Paris. Germany and its allies were not invited. Although many of the world's countries were represented, the Conference was dominated by the 'Big Three'. These were President Wilson of the USA, David Lloyd George of Britain and Georges Clemenceau of France.

The Big Three disagree
Unfortunately for Wilson, neither Lloyd George nor Clemenceau wanted to implement all of his Fourteen Points. France, in particular, wanted to punish Germany.

POLITICS, PEOPLE AND PREJUDICES

As the Conference developed, many of Wilson's ideas were either changed or ignored as Britain, France and Italy pursued their own interests. Wilson hoped that Europe could now be based on national self-determination (see Fact File): German-speaking Austria wanted to join with Germany, but Britain and France refused to allow this.

At the end of the Conference only some of Wilson's ideas had been accepted. This included the institution of the League of Nations. France and Britain, however, made sure Germany accepted responsibility for starting the war and for all the damage caused by it. In addition, the Germans were expected to pay £66 billion as reparations (compensation) to the Allies. In all, there were five peace treaties, each dealing with different parts of Europe and Turkey. The Treaty of Versailles dealt with Germany.

WHY DID THE US SENATE REJECT THE TREATY OF VERSAILLES?

Under the US Constitution the President has the right to sign treaties. However, before they become law, the President needs the support of two thirds of the Senate. Unfortunately for Wilson, the Senate rejected the Treaty of Versailles and US involvement in the League of Nations. It rejected the Treaty for several reasons.

Wilson at the Paris Peace Conference
Wilson had attended the Paris Peace Conference in person. It was usual to send a representative. It linked the Treaty directly to him and made it look like he was going ahead without the Senate's agreement.

Wilson's relations with the Republican Party
- During 1918 the Republican Party had gained a majority of seats in the Senate. Wilson was a Democrat. He needed the Republicans onside to get a majority vote in favour of the Treaty and the League of Nations. The Republicans criticised the outcome of the peace treaties because they did not match the Fourteen Points. They felt Britain and France had used the treaties to take revenge on Germany, not bring world peace.
- Wilson refused to compromise. He demanded that the USA accept all terms of the Treaty. The Republicans did not want to.

- The Republicans felt sidelined. Wilson had not invited any of them to be part of the US delegation to Paris. Neither had he kept the Republican Party informed of what he was doing there. Their Senate leader, Henry Cabot Lodge, became a very effective opponent of Wilson and the Treaty.

Wilson's health
In late September 1919 Wilson suffered a stroke that forced him out of politics for good. He had also suffered one whilst in Paris at the Peace Conference. He could no longer defend the Peace Settlement and the Senate rejected it on March 19, 1920.

SOURCE 2 **From** The USA and the World, 1917-1945, **by the British historian Peter Brett, written in 1997.**

'The decision to attend and participate in the peace settlement in person turned out to be a mistake.'

The USA did not sign the Treaty of Versailles or join the League of Nations. Instead, the USA made a separate peace treaty with Germany in 1920. When the Republican candidate, Warren Harding, won the 1920 presidential election he asked for a return to **normalcy**. He wanted the USA to concentrate on internal issues, not get involved in foreign affairs. The rejection of the Treaty of Versailles and Harding's election was meant to start a period of **isolationism** in foreign affairs.

normalcy
the idea that the USA should not get involved in European affairs

isolationism
the idea that the USA should concentrate on internal affairs

Questions

1. Study Source 1.
   a) How did the German policy of unrestricted U-boat warfare inspire this poster?
   b) How useful is this poster in explaining why the USA entered the First World War?
2. Study Source 2. Does this fully explain why the Treaty of Versailles was rejected by the US Senate? Give reasons for your answer.
3. Do you think Woodrow Wilson's involvement in the First World War and peace settlement was a success or a failure? Explain your answer.

Votes for women!

The USA is a democracy. However, until 1920 over half the adult population did not have the right to vote in federal (national) elections. Women were denied the vote to choose the President and Congress. However, before 1919, women could vote in certain parts of the USA. In 1869 the then territory of Wyoming gave women the vote for the first time. By 1911 six states had given women the right to vote in state and local elections. These were Wyoming, Colorado, Utah, Idaho, Washington and California. All these states were in the West. The demand for women's **suffrage** had a number of causes.

suffrage
the right to vote

WHY DID WOMEN DEMAND THE RIGHT TO VOTE IN NATIONAL ELECTIONS?

Women in other countries could vote
Throughout the English-speaking world in the late 19th and early 20th centuries, women demanded political equality with men. Countries like New Zealand and Australia were among the first to give women the vote. In the first decade of the 20th century the Suffragette movement in Britain also demanded votes for women. So women in the USA believed it was their right to vote.

Many were in favour of alcohol prohibition
Throughout the USA in the late 19th and early 20th centuries women were at the forefront of the movement for prohibition. In organisations such as the Women's Christian Temperance Union and the Anti-Saloon League (see p26), women were leaders of the campaign. In the Mid-West Mrs Carrie Nation attempted to end alcohol drinking by attacking bars with a hatchet (see Source 2, p26)! By giving women the vote, national prohibition would be more likely to be introduced because women would vote for pro-prohibition candidates.

Progressive social reforms
The period 1900 to 1920 was known as the Progressive Era in US history. This period was known for its social reforms. Laws were brought in to outlaw child labour and to give workers better working conditions. Also the rights of women were improved. Divorce laws were made easier and women gained more control over their own property once they got married. The demand for women's suffrage was part of this reform movement.

SOURCE 1

American women campaigning for the right to vote in 1905.

HOW DID WOMEN GET THE RIGHT TO VOTE IN NATIONAL ELECTIONS?

Women were at the forefront of the campaign. In 1890 the National American Women's Suffrage Association (NAWSA) was formed. In 1900 Carrie Chapman Catt took over the leadership of the NAWSA and made it into an effective national organisation. Also, in 1895, Mary Church Tyrell had formed the Colored Women's League, which supported the idea of votes for African-American women.

By 1911, the women's suffrage movement achieved its greatest triumph to date by getting the vote in California state elections. But 1912 was the major turning point. The National Women's Party was formed and women won the right to vote in Oregon, Kansas and Arizona. More importantly, Theodore Roosevelt's Bull Moose Progressive Party supported the idea of women's suffrage. Although Roosevelt did not win the presidential election it gave the whole idea of women's suffrage an important boost. Theodore Roosevelt had been a very successful President between 1901 and 1909 and had a large following in the USA.

SOURCE 2 A map showing when women got the vote in each US state, from 1875 to 1920. What information does it provide about the geographical development of women's suffrage?

Legend:
- 1869
- 1870
- 1893
- 1896
- 1910
- 1911
- 1912
- 1914
- 1917
- 1918
- 1920

By the outbreak of the First World War the movement was gaining widespread support. In 1917 the most populous state of the USA, New York, gave women the vote. Also, the House of Representatives in the US Congress created a Women's Suffrage Committee to examine the case for giving women the vote.

However, in 1918 the movement faced a big setback. The US Senate opposed an attempt to amend the Constitution to give women the vote.

constitutional amendment
a change to the constitution

Yet within a year another proposed **constitutional amendment** passed both the House of Representatives and the Senate. When three quarters of the 48 states supported the amendment, the US Constitution was changed. The 19th Amendment gave women the right to vote in national elections in 1920 for the first time.

SOURCE 3 The 19th Amendment to the United States Constitution, 1919. It was passed by the US Congress in June 1919 and became law in 1920.

'The rights of citizens of the United States to vote shall not be denied by the United States or by any state on account of sex. The Congress shall have power to enforce this amendment.'

FACT FILE

TIMELINE OF US WOMEN'S SUFFRAGE CAMPAIGN

1869	Territory of Wyoming gives votes to women
1895	National American Women's Suffrage Association (NAWSA) formed
1912	National Women's Party formed
1917	Women given the vote in New York State
1919	19th Amendment to the US Constitution passed by the US Congress gives the vote to all women over 21 years old
1920	Women allowed to vote in national elections for the first time

Questions

1. Study Source 1.
   a) How useful is this photograph as evidence of the campaign for women's suffrage in the USA in the period before 1919?
2. Study Source 3. How useful is this source to an historian studying the development of women's suffrage in the USA?
3. Explain why women in the USA demanded the right to vote in the early 20th century. Why was it a good time to do it?

Immigration controls – closing the door

One of the most famous statues in the USA is the Statue of Liberty. It stands on an island in New York harbour. Its inscription reads: 'Bring me your huddled masses yearning to be free'. The statue stands for the policy followed by the USA up to the 1920s – any person travelling from Europe could emigrate and start a new life in the USA. In the 1920s all that changed.

WHY WERE IMMIGRATION CONTROLS INTRODUCED?

Immigration controls were part of the White, Anglo-Saxon Protestant (WASP) backlash against foreign immigration. Most of the immigration in the years 1880 to 1920 had come from Central and Eastern Europe. These immigrants couldn't speak English when they arrived. They were also accused of bringing foreign political ideas to America such as **socialism** and **communism**.

From 1917 many Americans feared that European immigrants might bring ideas of social and political revolution similar to those that affected Russia in October 1917. In 1919 the USA suffered 'The Red Scare'. Police raids,

socialism
a political idea involving taking money from the rich to give to the poor to make society more equal

communism
a form of socialism where all business and property is owned by the government

> **SOURCE 2** "Thousands come here who never take the oath to the constitution. They pay allegiance to some other country. They fill jobs that belong to the loyal wage-earning citizens of America. They preach a doctrine that is dangerous and deadly to our government. They are a danger to us every day."
>
> From a speech on immigration by Senator Thomas Heflin of Alabama in 1921.

called Palmer Raids after the US **Attorney-General**, led to the arrest of hundreds of socialists and communists. Most of these were foreign-born immigrants.

Attorney-General
the highest law officer in the US Government

In 1920 two Italian immigrants were accused of the murder of two men in a robbery. They were Nicola Sacco and Bartolomeo Vanzetti. Both were **anarchists**. They had also avoided military service in the First World War. Although evidence against them was very limited, both were found guilty.

anarchist
a person who does not believe in any form of government

Eventually, in 1927, they were executed. Their supporters believed they were only found guilty because of their political views. However, recent evidence would suggest that Sacco was actually guilty.

WHAT FORM DID IMMIGRATION CONTROLS TAKE?

Two acts of Congress were passed: the Emergency Quota Act (1921) and the National Origins or Johnson-Reed Act (1924). The 1921 Act was an emergency measure. It limited immigration to 357,000 people per year. It also introduced quotas (limits) on immigration from certain countries. The quota was limited to 3 per cent of the number of immigrants from each country, based on the 1910 census. This benefited those

SOURCE 1

Immigrants on a European steamship catch their first glimpse of New York Harbor in July, 1922.

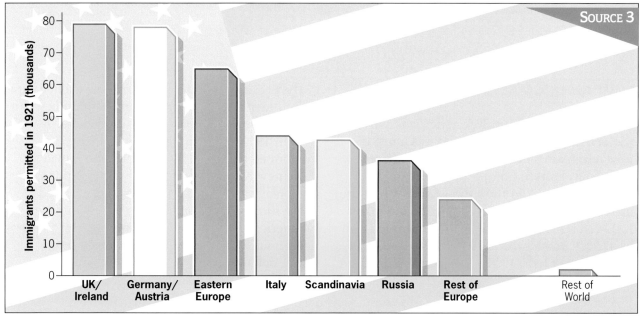

Immigrants permitted in 1921 (thousands)

UK/Ireland	
Germany/Austria	
Eastern Europe	
Italy	
Scandinavia	
Russia	
Rest of Europe	
Rest of World	

This bar chart shows the number of immigrants admitted to the USA in 1921.

from countries in northwest Europe because more had entered the USA from that area in 1910 than from other parts of the world. The method of calculating the immigration quotas was so complicated that it took until 1929 to work them out!

The Johnson-Reed Act of 1924 made all temporary immigration measures permanent. From 1924 the annual number of immigrants was cut to 165,000. The Act also reduced the quotas to two per cent of the number from each country, based on the 1890 census. This benefited immigrants from northwest Europe even more, for the same reasons as in 1921. By 1927 annual immigration was limited to 150,000 per year.

INVESTIGATE...
What hardships did immigrants in the 1920s face before and after arriving in the USA? Visit
www.historychannel.com/exhibits/ellisisle

An American cartoon, published in 1921 after the passage of the Emergency Quota Act. The person in the top hat is 'Uncle Sam', who represents the USA.

Questions

1. Study Source 2.
   a) What "dangerous and deadly doctrine" do you think immigrants supported, according to Senator Heflin?
   b) What reason does the Senator give for introducing immigration controls?
2. Study Source 3. How did the American government make sure that most immigrants from 1921 came from west and central Europe?
3. Study Source 4. How reliable is the cartoon as evidence of the immigration controls introduced in 1921?
4. What do you regard as the most important reason for the introduction of immigration controls in the USA in the early 1920s? Give reasons for your answer.

Ku Klux Klan – the politics of hate

NEW AMERICA AND OLD AMERICA

In the early 20th century America was a divided society. One half of the division was made up of new immigrants from all over Europe. People from Italy, Eastern Europe and Germany had gone to the USA in their thousands. When they arrived they couldn't speak English, and many followed religions such as Catholicism, Judaism and Orthodox Christianity.

The other half of the division was a different America. This comprised British descendants, or those from a Protestant, Anglo-Saxon background. They were descended from the original settlers of the 17th and 18th centuries. They were known as WASPS (White, Anglo-Saxon Protestants), and they wanted to maintain their control of politics and society. From this group came the organisation known as the Ku Klux Klan.

HOW DID THE KU KLUX KLAN GROW FROM 1915?

The Ku Klux Klan had originally been formed after the American Civil War in 1866, in Pulaski, Tennessee. It was a secret society with the aim of protecting whites in the Old South who had fought for the Confederate States in the Civil War. Their main opponents were African-Americans recently freed from slavery and their northern supporters.

Confederate States
a breakaway group of 11 states in the southeast of the USA. Their decision to form a separate state led to the American Civil War of 1861-1865

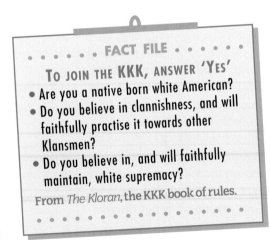

. . . . . **FACT FILE** . . . . .
To join the **KKK**, answer 'Yes'
• Are you a native born white American?
• Do you believe in clannishness, and will faithfully practise it towards other Klansmen?
• Do you believe in, and will faithfully maintain, white supremacy?
From *The Kloran*, the KKK book of rules.

They operated in the southern states. They kept their identity secret by wearing white robes. But by 1877 the KKK had gone into decline.

In 1915 William Simmons of Georgia reformed the Klan. The people who joined the new KKK were inspired by one of the most popular Hollywood films of the time, called *The Birth of a Nation*. It was a film about the American Civil War and its immediate aftermath. The Klan was shown in a heroic way, defending the WASP population of the Old South.

Although Simmons was responsible for re-founding the KKK, it was Edward Young Clarke and Mrs Elizabeth Tyler who were most responsible for its growth. They began an advertising campaign selling membership with the KKK robes for $10.

Who did the Ku Klux Klan oppose?
The KKK of the 1920s did not just oppose African-Americans. They also disliked what they saw as any foreign influence or threat to their society. These groups included Jews, Catholics, bootleggers (see pp28-29) and socialists. Their convictions were so widely supported that by 1924 the KKK had four million members spread across the USA – not just in the Old South.

SOURCE 1

A member of the Ku Klux Klan outside the Capitol Building in Washington DC.

HOW MUCH INFLUENCE DID THE KKK HAVE IN THE 1920S?

The KKK was able to influence the election of politicians across the USA. In the northeast state of Maine, the Attorney-General spoke out against the Klan. The Klan promptly had him removed from office. Elsewhere, Governors, State Assemblymen and even Senators in the US Congress were under Klan influence.

In 1924 a Catholic, Al Smith, stood for the position of Democratic Party presidential candidate. The Klan opposed him – this was very influential in his defeat.

In the Old South the KKK made sure that African-Americans remained second-class citizens. To achieve this they used intimidation and terror, including lynchings. Perhaps the Klan's greatest influence came in its support for limits on immigration (see p15). By 1924, immigration had been limited by the federal government in a way that favoured people from northwest Europe.

lynching
hanging someone without a trial

WHY DID THE KU KLUX KLAN DECLINE RAPIDLY BETWEEN 1925 AND 1929?

In 1924 the Klan had four million members nationwide. By 1929 the numbers had fallen to just under 200,000.

A major reason was the scandal surrounding David Stephenson, Grand Dragon of the KKK in Indiana. In 1925 he was convicted of the rape and murder of a woman on a train. Other Klan members were convicted of corruption and bribery of public officials.

This adverse publicity caused great damage, in particular because the Klan regarded itself as upholding moral, Christian values of honesty and good living

The decline of the Klan was also, in part, due to its success. The introduction of immigration controls in 1921 and 1924 achieved many of its supporters aims.

SOURCE 2 A lynching in Marion, Indiana, in 1930. Indiana is a Midwest state that fought for the North in the Civil War. The two African-Americans had been accused of murder but did not have a trial.

THE KU KLUX KLAN

The organisation took its name from the Greek word for circle, *kyklos*. Members of the organisation were meant to be secret. At meetings they wore hooded robes. A feature of Klan meetings was to burn a large cross, symbolising their support for Protestant Christianity. The rule book of the KKK was called the Kloran (after the Muslim holy book Koran). Members were organised into Klaverns. The KKK had a clear structure, like an army, with members known as Kleagles and Grand Dragon. The overall leader was called the Imperial Wizard. Because of its secrecy it was also known as 'The Invisible Empire'.

Questions

1. Study Source 1. Given the location and time of day, how does this photograph show that the KKK was influential in the USA?
2. Study Source 2.
   a) Describe the white crowd's attitude towards the lynching.
   b) Explain how events like this prevented African-Americans from demanding equal civil rights with whites.
3. How did the Ku Klux Klan affect life in the USA in the 1920s?

BIG CITY AMERICA AND SMALL TOWN AMERICA

America in the 1920s was a rapidly changing society. Economic prosperity created big cities like New York and Chicago. Some had skyscraper buildings. New music such as jazz and dances like the Charleston and the Black Bottom became popular in cities across the country.

However, this vision of 1920s America was very different to that of small town and farming America. People in these areas disliked and distrusted the changes in the cities. Partly in reaction to the modern changes affecting big city America, a religious revival took place. This revival was amongst white, Protestant America. Using radio, Aimee Semple McPherson won a large following for her 'Four Square Gospel Hour' from the Angeles Temple in Los Angeles, California. Other Protestant preachers toured the country spreading the word of the Bible. One of the most famous was a reformed alcoholic called Billy Sunday. He told people to follow the Bible and give up the 'demon drink'.

SOURCE 1

Anti-evolution books enjoyed record sales in Dayton during the Scopes Monkey Trial.

WHY WAS THE SCOPES 'MONKEY TRIAL' SO FAMOUS?

John T. Scopes was a biology teacher in a high school in Tennessee. In that state it was illegal to teach the idea of evolution. Instead children were taught that the human race came directly from Adam and Eve, who were created by God to live in the Garden of Eden.

Scopes deliberately taught his students the idea that man evolved from other creatures, in particular distant members of the ape family. As a result he was put on trial in the small town of Dayton, Tennessee, in 1925. His trial became known as the Scopes 'Monkey Trial'.

The trial caught the public imagination because Scopes was defended by one of America's most famous lawyers, Clarence Darrow. The main prosecution witness was William Jennings Bryan.

SOURCE 2

Darrow and Bryan at the Scopes Monkey Trial.

At one stage in the trial the temperature inside the courtroom was so high, and the number of spectators inside it so many, that the judge took the court outside. Here Darrow called Bryan to the witness stand. The dialogue that followed represented a turning point in the trial and was crucial in bringing public opinion over to Darrow's side.

Q: "You have given considerable study to the Bible, haven't you, Mr. Bryan?"

A: *"Yes, sir; I have tried to..."*

Q: "Do you claim then that everything in the Bible should be literally interpreted?"

A: *"I believe everything in the Bible should be accepted as it is given there..."*

Darrow continued to question Bryan on the reality of stories such as Jonah and the whale and the Tower of Babel. Bryan began to have more difficulty answering.

Q: "Do you think the earth was made in six days?"

A: *"Not six days of 24 hours... My impression is they were periods..."*

Q: "Now, if you call those 'periods', they may have been a very long time?"

A: *"They might have been."*

Q: "The creation might have been going on for a very long time?"

A: *"It might have continued for millions of years..."*

He had been Democrat presidential candidate in 1896, 1900 and 1908, and Secretary of State under Woodrow Wilson (1913-1917).

fundamentalist
a belief that the Bible's account of creation is the only accurate version

Clarence Darrow was able to discredit Bryan's fundamentalist religious ideas. Scopes was found guilty, but the Tennessee Supreme Court reversed the decision. Even so, many states still had laws that allowed only the Bible's literal interpretation of creation to be taught.

A magazine advert for a Hollywood film on the Scopes 'Monkey Trial' called *Inherit the Wind*. The film was released in 1960.

THEY CLASH HEAD-ON IN HISTORY'S MOST DRAMATIC TRIAL BY JURY!

SPENCER TRACY / FREDRIC MARCH / GENE KELLY

in Stanley Kramer's Production of INHERIT THE WIND

UNITED ARTISTS

with Dick York · Donna Anderson · Harry Morgan · Claude Akins and Florence Eldridge

Based upon the play by JEROME LAWRENCE and ROBERT E. LEE · Screenplay by NATHAN E. DOUGLAS and HAROLD JACOB SMITH · Produced and Directed by STANLEY KRAMER

Questions

1. Study Sources 1 and 2. Both these photographs were taken in Dayton, Tennessee during the Scopes 'Monkey Trial'. Which one do you think would be more useful to a historian writing about the trial? Give reasons for your answer.
2. Study Source 3. How does Clarence Darrow get William Jennings Bryan to accept that the theory of evolution was possible?
3. Study Source 4. 'Because the film was made in 1960 it is of little use to a historian writing about the Scopes 'Monkey Trial'.' Do you agree or disagree with this view? Explain your answer.
4. Study pp14-15, as well as this section. Explain the ways in which many white, Protestant Americans tried to stop changes taking place in American society during the 1920s.

Was the USA isolationist?

US FOREIGN POLICY IN THE 1920S AND 1930S

Following the rejection of the Treaty of Versailles, the USA refused to take part in the League of Nations. President Harding (1921-1923) announced that the USA would return to normalcy. This meant that the USA would concentrate on internal affairs. But to what extent was the USA actually isolationist throughout this period? On many occasions the USA did, in fact, take part in important world events.

FAMINE RELIEF IN EUROPE, 1920

The USA set up the Famine Relief Administration in 1920. Its aim was to help famine victims in Eastern Europe, and especially Russia, which was struggling amidst a civil war. Future President Herbert Hoover was very successful in administering famine relief.

THE WASHINGTON NAVAL TREATY FEBRUARY, 1922

One of President Wilson's Fourteen Points (see p10) was the reduction of all armaments. In Washington DC, in 1922, the USA hosted a conference which reduced naval armaments in the Pacific Ocean. The USA, Britain and Japan all agreed to limit their number of battleships in the Pacific region. Japan had already decided to build battleships above the limit imposed in Washington. Following this Treaty, Japan converted some of these to aircraft carriers.

THE DAWES AND YOUNG PLANS, 1924 AND 1929

In the 1920s one of the big problems facing Europe was Germany's reparations payments to the Allies. In 1923 Germany failed to keep up its payments, so French and Belgian troops occupied the industrial area of western Germany called the Ruhr. This occupation helped create hyperinflation in Germany, whose currency became virtually worthless. In an international conference in 1924 the unofficial US representative, Charles Dawes, organised a plan to end the crisis. US loans to Germany enabled Germany to pay reparations to the wartime Allies. The Dawes Plan brought about the temporary economic recovery of Germany in the 1920s.

In 1929 US delegate Owen Young helped reorganise German reparations payments. The time for payment was extended until the 1980s! This was called the Young Plan.

An American cartoon about European war debts in the 1920s, produced in 1924.

THE KELLOGG-BRIAND PACT OF 1928

In 1928, Robert Kellogg, the US Secretary of State (Foreign Secretary), and the Foreign Minister of France, Aristide Briand, signed an agreement. This declared that the countries that signed it would reject war as a way of settling disputes. Eventually 15 other countries signed the Pact. Although the US Senate accepted the treaty, it also voted for the building of 15 large warships in the same year.

RELATIONS WITH LATIN AMERICA

Although the USA would not send troops to Europe after the First World War, this did not stop US interference in Latin America. Under the Monroe Doctrine of 1823, the USA declared all the Americas – not just North America – were within its area of influence. The USA sent troops to Nicaragua from 1912 to 1925, and from 1926 to 1933. Haiti was under US military government from 1915 to 1934, and the Dominican Republic was occupied between 1916 and 1924.

In 1933 FD Roosevelt became President. He started the Good Neighbour Policy towards Latin America. He wanted the USA to develop more trade links. From 1934 US troops were withdrawn from Latin America. The USA gave up the right to intervene in Cuba. In place of active intervention came trade agreements in Montevideo, Uruguay (1934), Buenos Aires, Argentina (1936) and Lima, Peru (1938).

CRISIS IN ASIA, CHINA AND JAPAN, 1931-1940

Throughout most of the 20th century the USA had supported an open-door policy towards China. This meant that any country had the right to trade with China.

In 1931 Japan invaded and occupied the north Chinese province of Manchuria.

Although the League of Nations condemned Japanese actions, President Hoover refused to intervene. In 1937 Japan invaded the rest of China. Again the US did not intervene. However, FDR did not stop US volunteers joining the Chinese air force.

It was only after the Japanese occupation of French Indo-China (modern day Vietnam, Cambodia and Laos) in 1940 that FDR took action in the form of economic sanctions.

economic sanctions *to stop trading with a country to punish it, destabilising its economy*

THE NEUTRALITY ACTS, 1935-1937

By the mid-1930s fears of war began to develop in Europe. Hitler had come to power in Germany in 1933, determined to destroy the Treaty of Versailles. In 1935 Italian Dictator Mussolini invaded Ethiopia (known as Abyssinia) in East Africa. In 1936 the Spanish Civil War began. To help prevent US involvement in overseas problems, Congress passed the Neutrality Acts of 1935 and 1937. These prevented the USA from giving aid to anyone engaged in an overseas war.

SOURCE 3

An American cartoon on the outbreak of the Spanish Civil War in 1936. The person in the picture is Uncle Sam.

Questions

1. Study Source 1.
   a) What statement is the cartoon trying to make about Europe trying to pay back American loans?
   b) How reliable is this cartoon as evidence of war debt problems facing European countries in the mid-1920s?
2. Study Source 2. How useful is this cartoon to an historian writing about why the USA did not get involved in the war between China and Japan?
3. What reasons can you give for the failure of the USA to intervene in the Spanish Civil War?

The causes of economic prosperity in the 1920s

A CHICKEN IN EVERY POT, A CAR IN EVERY GARAGE!

In the 1928 presidential election the Republican candidate – and future President – Herbert Hoover, said that the USA had become the first society to have ended poverty. He was able to make this statement because most Americans at the time believed they had created a society that would have permanent economic prosperity. What were the causes of this prosperity?

AMERICA'S NATURAL RESOURCES

The USA had abundant natural resources upon which prosperity was built. It contained large coalfields in states such as Kentucky, Pennsylvania and West Virginia. It also possessed abundant oil reserves in California, Oklahoma and Texas. Iron ore came from Minnesota and other metals like lead, copper and zinc were found across the Rocky Mountain region. In addition, the whole western region of the country was covered by large forests.

The 15 millionth Ford Model T rolls off the production line.

THE IMPACT OF THE FIRST WORLD WAR

The war had acted as a great boost to the economy. Countries like Britain and France placed huge orders for armaments with US firms. This demand helped the growth of industries such as iron and steel and engineering

Also, by 1918, the USA had emerged from the war as the world's largest economy. Millions of British and French men had been killed or wounded, and both their countries owed the USA millions of dollars in war debts. By comparison, the USA had lost only 60,000 men and was untouched by war damage.

MASS PRODUCTION

Perhaps the most important reason for US prosperity in the 1920s was the development of mass production manufacturing techniques. Carmaker Henry Ford in Detroit, Michigan, pioneered the idea with the production of his Model 'T' Ford car.

A moving production line was introduced. The basic frame, or chassis, of a car was placed on it. As it moved through the factory, workers added the wheels, body and engine until it left the production line as a finished car.

This method quickened production and cut costs. In 1914 a Model T cost $850. By 1926 it was $295. It was so successful that other industries adopted the method.

SOURCE 1   A Ford advert from 1923.

More than a Car
Ford
A National Institution

THE GROWTH OF THE CAR INDUSTRY

The car transformed America. With increasingly cheap motor vehicles being produced, ordinary Americans could now travel like they had never done before. The car industry led to the growth of other industries: the electrical industry for lights; the rubber industry for tyres; engineering firms for brakes. Car development also encouraged the development of a modern road system.

NEW CONSUMER GOODS

The 1920s also saw the rapid rise in the sale of other consumer goods. Radios were sold by the million and became the most popular form of entertainment. Telephones also sold rapidly. Refrigerators, vacuum cleaners, and washing machines became regular features of American homes.

HIRE PURCHASE, CREDIT AND ADVERTISING

To enable Americans to buy consumer goods, companies developed hire purchase or credit schemes. This meant a person could acquire something for a down payment of a fraction of the total cost. They could then pay off, in instalments, the remaining money while continuing to use the product. This development greatly increased sales.

To encourage consumers to buy, advertising became widespread. On billboards, in cinemas and newspapers, Americans were constantly bombarded with the call to buy more goods.

THE ECONOMIC POLICY OF THE REPUBLICAN GOVERNMENTS

From 1921 to 1933 the USA was governed by the Republican Party. It followed a **laissez-faire** economic policy. President Calvin Coolidge (1923-1929) said, "The business of America is business". The government did everything it could to encourage business to grow. **Secretary to the Treasury**, Andrew Mellon, lowered company and personal taxes. This encouraged more consumer spending.

laissez-faire
minimum government intervention in economic affairs

Secretary to the Treasury
US equivalent to Chancellor of the Exchequer

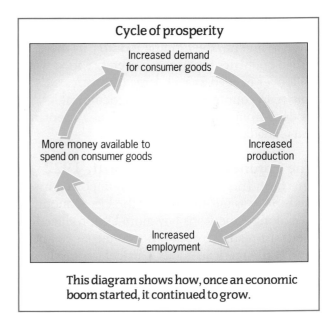

Cycle of prosperity

Increased demand for consumer goods → Increased production → Increased employment → More money available to spend on consumer goods →

This diagram shows how, once an economic boom started, it continued to grow.

SOURCE 2	1920	1929
Cars produced	9 million	26 million
km of roads	620,000	1 million
Radios	60,000	10 million
Telephones	13 million	20 million

Areas where the US economy boomed in the 1920s.

SOURCE 3	Gross National Product in the USA
1921	$74 billion
1926	$97 billion
1929	$104 billion

Gross National Product is the total annual amount of goods and services produced by an economy.

Questions

1. Study Source 1.
   a) What information does the advert contain to help you understand why the USA was prosperous in the 1920s?
   b) Does it offer a full explanation why? Give reasons for your answer.
2. Study Source 2. Explain why there was such a big increase in these particular areas of the economy from 1920 to 1929.
3. Explain how the increase in Gross National Product can lead to greater prosperity for the whole economy.

Who missed out on prosperity in the 1920s?

The 1920s are usually portrayed as a period of economic prosperity in the USA. However, this was not the case for US farmers or African-Americans.

WHY DID FARMERS DO SO BADLY?

Throughout the decade farmers faced falling prices for their goods. Tens of thousands of them faced hardship. Six million left the land to work in cities. Why?

The impact of the end of the First World War

During the First World War the USA supplied the Allies in Europe with food. Once the war came to an end, the farming industry in the Allied countries began to recover. US food was no longer needed in such large quantities. Also, European countries could buy agricultural produce from other countries such as Argentina and Canada.

The Fordney-McCumber Tariff, 1922

This tariff (tax) on foreign goods imported into the USA was meant to boost the US economy by making Americans buy more US-produced goods. Instead, it forced other countries to put tariffs on American goods, particularly food. This meant that US farmers found it more difficult to sell their produce overseas.

Mechanisation

During the 1920s the US agricultural industry became mechanised. New machines, like the combine harvester, were able to do the work of several men. Tractors replaced horses. As agricultural production rose, employment in farming fell.

Overproduction

With mechanisation came a great increase in farm production. As production rose, so farm prices fell. This was made worse by the development of synthetic fibres like rayon. This provided strong competition for traditional fibres like cotton. The average farm income in 1929 was $273. The average industrial income was $750.

SOURCE 1	Difference in price of some agricultural goods, 1920 and 1932.	
	1920	**1932**
Wheat	$1.82 a bushel	38 cents a bushel
Maize (Corn)	61 cents a bushel	32 cents a bushel
Cotton	16 cents a pound	6 cents a pound

SOURCE 2 An American cartoon from the 1920s. What statement is it trying to make about the US economy in the 1920s?

Lack of government support

Supporters of farmers in the US Congress tried to help raise farm prices. In 1924 the Farm Relief Bill (or McNary-Haugen Bill) was introduced. It planned to make the federal government control farm prices. This would prevent prices falling. The same bill was put forward in 1924, 1927 and 1928. On each occasion the President, Calvin Coolidge, used his veto to stop the bill from becoming law (see Source 3). He believed in laissez-faire economics.

SOURCE 3 Adapted from a speech by President Coolidge against the McNary-Haugen Bill.

"Instead of undertaking a method of marketing which will sell goods at a profit, it plans to sell them at a loss. This goes against the government's economic principles, which require farmers to produce only what can be sold at a profit. They should not waste soil by producing what can be sold only at a loss."

WHY DID AFRICAN-AMERICANS MISS OUT?

Farmers were not the only section of US society to miss out on the boom years of the 1920s. At this time the majority of African-Americans lived in the Old South, where their ancestors had been slaves. Most worked on small farms, which they rented from white landlords. They received seeds and farmland in return for a share of the crop. They were called sharecroppers, and lived in poverty.

To make matters worse, the Old South states had a system known as segregation. Whites and blacks were forced to live entirely separate lives. Housing, education and transport separated the white and black communities. There were even separate drinking fountains and toilets (see p58). Separate African-American facilities were usually inferior to those for whites. If anyone attempted to improve African-American rights and conditions they faced intimidation from the Ku Klux Klan (see p16).

HOW DID LIFE CHANGE FOR AFRICAN-AMERICANS IN THE 1920S?

One major change was the 'Great Migration'. Between 1915 and 1925, 1.25 million blacks took the train north to cities like Chicago and New York. Between 1910 and 1930 the black population of Chicago increased from 44,000 to 234,000. In New York City in the same period the black population grew from 91,000 to 328,000.

Even though they lived in the North, African-Americans still faced discrimination. They lived in separate black areas (Harlem in New York and the South Side in Chicago).

But here, African-Americans developed their own form of music, known as jazz. This became the most popular form of music in the 1920s. Louis Armstrong, an African-American musician, was one of the most popular entertainers of the decade (see p31).

Other African-Americans became important writers and novelists.

WHO WAS MARCUS GARVEY?

One of the most important African-Americans in the 1920s was Marcus Garvey. Brought up in the British West Indies, in 1914 he founded the Universal Negro Improvement Association (UNIA). It aimed to help African-Americans get a better life. By 1920 it had two million members. It created black-owned businesses. African-Americans were encouraged to use these. Unfortunately, Garvey was arrested by the FBI in 1923 for mail fraud. He was fined $1,000 and sent to prison for five years.

> ### · · · FACT FILE · · ·
> ### THE AIMS OF THE UNIA
> - To support Negro (black) nationhood by the liberation of Africa from European colonial rule
> - To encourage Negroes to make a better life for themselves (racial self-help)
> - To inspire Negroes to respect their race and origins (racial self-respect)
> - To print all news of interest to the Negro

Questions

1. Study Source 2. How useful is the cartoon as evidence of the position of farmers in the 1920s?
2. Study Source 3.
   a) What reason does President Coolidge give for opposing the McNary-Haugen Bill?
   b) How reliable is his speech as evidence of why the Bill was not introduced?
3. Study Source 4.
   a) How does 'The Jazz Singer' show racial discrimination against African-Americans?
   b) How does the film suggest that African-American influence in America was growing in the 1920s? Explain your answer
4. How was the situation of farmers in the 1920s different to that of African-Americans in the 1920s? Explain your answer.

SOURCE 4

A poster for the first Hollywood film to have sound, *The Jazz Singer* (1927). It starred a Jewish American singer, called Al Jolson. When singing on stage, Jolson coloured his skin black to play an African-American 'jazz singer'.

National prohibition, 1920 to 1933

END THE DEMON DRINK!

On January 16, 1920, the USA began 'The Noble Experiment'. From midnight on that day the manufacture, sale and consumption of alcohol was illegal across the whole country. This law was introduced in 1919 by the 18th Amendment to the US Constitution. This was backed up by the Volstead Act, passed in the same year. The Amendment had only barred what it called 'intoxicating liquor'. The Volstead Act then defined 'intoxicating liquor' as any drink containing more than 0.5 per cent alcohol. Most beers contained three per cent to five per cent alcohol. Whiskey contained 35 per cent alcohol.

WHY WAS NATIONAL PROHIBITION INTRODUCED?

By 1919 most US states had already banned the consumption of alcohol. These were mainly located in the Old South and the West. The campaign was led by two main groups. The Women's Christian Temperance Union (WCTU) opposed alcohol on moral and religious grounds. It was formed in 1875. In 1893 it was joined by another powerful group, the Anti-Saloon League (ASL). The ASL was led by a very effective organiser called Wayne Wheeler. He was able to organise successful campaigns at

WCTU supporter Mrs Carrie Nation with bible and hatchet in 1910. She used the hatchet to smash saloon bars.

state level, and in 1907 Oklahoma became 'dry'. In 1909 Tennessee followed (see map).

WHY WAS PROHIBITION SUPPORTED?

Moral reasons
Supporters of prohibition believed drinking alcohol ruined family life and caused child abuse. Working men were portrayed as taking their weekly pay packet to a saloon and drinking it away. They returned home penniless. Alcohol was also seen to encourage drunkenness and family violence.

A map showing the spread of statewide and local prohibition in 1919.

SOURCE 1

Statewide prohibition
Local prohibition

PROSPERITY, PROHIBITION AND POPULAR CULTURE

Religious reasons

Moral reasons were linked to religious reasons. It was seen as unchristian to drink because it encouraged this immoral behaviour. It was also seen as demeaning to women as saloons were almost always for men only.

Commercial reasons

John D Rockefeller, one of America's richest businessmen, was a leading figure in the movement against alcohol. Businessmen believed drunkenness created major health and safety issues at work, where a drunken worker could cause damage to machinery. Drinking also reduced the work rate of employees.

SOURCE 3

Adapted from *The Long Thirst*, by the historian Thomas Coffey, 1975.

'John D Rockefeller was a known contributor to the dry cause. He believed that the nation's workers would be more productive if beer and liquor could be withheld from them. Rockefeller poured at least $350,000 into the Anti-Saloon League before 1920.'

The impact of the First World War

The war gave an enormous boost to the national prohibition campaign. The use of grain to make alcohol was seen as a waste. Grain was needed to feed the USA at a time of shortage. Alcohol was also thought to degrade military discipline. Even today it is banned in the US Navy.

An even more powerful reason to support prohibition was the growth of anti-German feeling. The major beer producers in the USA were mainly of German origin: Pabst, Budweiser and Schlitz. To drink German beer after the nation had been at war with Germany was seen as unpatriotic.

Racial reasons

Another very persuasive argument in favour of prohibition was the close association of alcohol with new immigrant groups into the USA. Drinking was associated with the Irish, Germans and Italians. These groups had settled in big cities. Rural and small town America was still predominantly white, Protestant and descended from English and Scottish stock. National prohibition was seen as a way of preserving their White, Anglo-Saxon Protestant (WASP) way of life.

SOURCE 4

A poster produced by the Anti-Saloon League in 1918. What statement is it trying to make?

INVESTIGATE...

Build your own timeline of key events leading to the introduction of national prohibition in 1920, starting in 1875. Use information at http://www.historychannel.com/classroom.

Questions

1. Study Source 2. Compare the methods of Carrie Nation and the poster in Source 4. Which method do you think was most effective in getting across the message to ban alcohol drinking?
2. Study Source 3. Does the evidence in this source fully explain why national prohibition was introduced? Explain your answer.
3. Study Source 4. What reasons are given in the poster to support national prohibition?
4. What do you regard as the most important reason for the introduction of national prohibition in 1920? Give reasons for your answer.

'The Noble Experiment' fails

National prohibition was introduced by the 18th Amendment to the US Constitution in 1919. As the first ten amendments are generally regarded as part of the original Constitution, that document had only been changed eight times in 130 years! Yet in 1933 another amendment, the 21st, reversed the 18th and ended national prohibition.

Why had such a major change taken place in such a short time?

MANY ORDINARY AMERICANS IGNORED PROHIBITION

From the very first day many Americans refused to accept the change in law. Across the country thousands of illegal drinking rooms, known as 'speakeasies', were set up. It was still very easy to buy alcohol. It didn't help that President Harding (1921-1923) was widely known to drink alcohol regularly in the White House.

Throughout the 1920s prohibition became the most ignored law in US History. When alcohol producers shut down it was very easy to find alternative supplies.

IT WAS VERY DIFFICULT TO ENFORCE

When alcohol producers shut down it was very easy to find alternative supplies.

booze
alcoholic drink

brewery
a place for making beer and lager

distillery
a place for making gin, whiskey and brandy. These drinks were known as hard liquor

Canada and Mexico still produced alcohol. It was very easy to smuggle **booze** across the 3000-mile border with Canada or the 1500-mile border with Mexico.

It was also very easy to obtain the ingredients for booze. Industrial alcohol used in chemical manufacture could be purchased and grain was easily available. Ordinary Americans created their own 'bath tub' **breweries** or **distilleries**.

The Treasury Department of Government had the job of enforcing prohibition. It only had 3000 agents for the whole of the USA. On average these agents were paid only $2500 a year. As a result it was easy to bribe them to prevent prosecution.

THE INVOLVEMENT OF ORGANISED CRIME

Illegal booze became a multi-million dollar industry in the 1920s. It attracted the involvement of organised crime groups like the Mafia. These groups were based in most big cities. The centre of the illegal trade in booze (known as 'bootlegging') was Chicago. This city is close to Canada and was a hub of the major railroad and road network for the centre of America.

Rival gangs fought each other for control of the bootlegging industry. Ordinary Americans were outraged at the level of violence associated with bootlegging. The most successful and notorious gangster involved was Italian American Al Capone. He bribed the police, judges and local politicians to keep his illegal empire of bootlegging, gambling and prostitution going.

ALPHONSE 'SCARFACE' CAPONE (1899-1947)

Probably the most celebrated gangster of the 1920s, Capone rose to prominence in Chicago early in the decade. In 1924 he eliminated his major rival, Dion O'Banion. This began a gang war in Chicago, which lasted until the St. Valentine's Day Massacre of 1929 when Capone had seven of O'Banion's men gunned down in a garage. In 1927 Capone's 'business empire' was worth $27 million. This came from bootlegging, prostitution and gambling. He also controlled local politicians, including the Mayor of Chicago. Capone was finally arrested and imprisoned in 1931 for tax evasion. During the trial he tried to bribe the jury but was eventually found guilty and served 11 years in jail.

WHY DID PROHIBITION END?

Support of and opposition to prohibition split the Democrat Party in 1928. The anti-prohibition group put forward Catholic Irish American Al Smith as their presidential candidate. Dry Democrats from the South and West opposed Smith.

Women, who had been prominent in the campaign for prohibition, now led the campaign for its end. The Association against the Prohibition Amendment claimed 'The Noble Experiment' had increased not reduced domestic violence.

In 1929 President Hoover created the Wickersham Commission into Prohibition. It supported prohibition but said that it was impossible to enforce.

When the Depression began many argued that ending national prohibition would create jobs, particularly in the manufacture of booze.

In the 1932 presidential campaign Franklin D Roosevelt (FDR) supported the end of national prohibition. When he became president he passed the Beer Act of 1933, which raised the level of alcohol mentioned in the Volstead Act. Later in 1933 the 21st Amendment was passed. These allowed states to choose whether or not they wanted prohibition. 'Happy days are here again!', declared FDR's campaign song.

An anti-prohibition demonstration.

Figures produced by the Philadelphia Police Department, 1920 to 1925. Philadelphia was a city of 150,000 in Pennsylvania. The totals included arrests for drunkenness, disorderly conduct, alcoholism and being a bootleg driver.

Alcohol-related arrests (thousands)

Year	Arrests
1920	20.4
1921	27.6
1922	44.7
1923	54.1
1924	55.8
1925	58.5

Questions

1. Study Source 1.
   a) What reason do the demonstrators give for opposing national prohibition?
   b) Does this photograph fully explain why national prohibition was opposed across America?
2. Study Source 2.
   a) Can you give reasons for the rise in statistics associated with alcohol during the early years of national prohibition?
   b) Does the data show that national prohibition failed across America? Give reasons for your answer.
3. Explain why you think prohibition failed in the USA during the 1920s. Use the sources and information on pages 28-31.

The rise of popular culture

The 1920s was a period of great change in US society. The decade was associated with changes in music, dance and fashion. However, the dominant feature of the decade was the rise in importance of the motion picture.

WHY WAS HOLLYWOOD SO IMPORTANT IN THE 1920S?

Films had been made in the USA since the beginning of the twentieth century. Originally the centre of filmmaking was around New York City. However, by 1914 the industry had moved to southern California. Hollywood was a suburb of Los Angeles. This area was popular with filmmakers because of its excellent climate, which was sunny and warm for most of the year. It was also close to mountains and deserts where films could be shot 'on location'.

By 1920 every American town had at least one cinema. It was the main form of entertainment for most Americans. Cinema was cheap and offered a variety of films, from comedy to adventure. Film actors became household names. The most popular comedy star in 1920 was British-born Charlie Chaplin. He usually played a tramp. His popularity came from the fact that he played an ordinary man who challenged authority.

In adventure films, Douglas Fairbanks played pirates and adventurers. In romance, the first great 'heart throb' of film was Rudolf Valentino. In the film *The Son of the Sheik* he played the strong, handsome leading man.

The most influential film produced by Hollywood was the 1915 *Birth of a Nation*. It dealt with the American Civil War. It was responsible for the rapid rise in popularity of the Ku Klux Klan.

A revolutionary change affected Hollywood in 1927. The first film using sound was produced. It was *The Jazz Singer*, starring Al Jolson (see p25). From 1927 silent films gave way to 'talkies'. The following year, 1928, saw the award of the first 'Oscars' for success in films.

By 1930 Hollywood stars were the best-known people in the USA. Ordinary Americans began to copy their hairstyles and fashion and even the way they talked and walked.

SOURCE 1

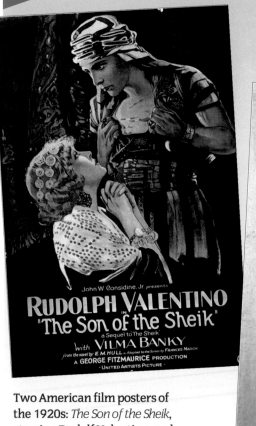

Two American film posters of the 1920s: *The Son of the Sheik*, starring Rudolf Valentino, and *The Kid*, starring Charlie Chaplin.

HOW DID FASHION CHANGE IN THE 1920S?

The 1920s was a decade of freedom for American women. In 1919 they received the right to vote. The prosperity of the 1920s brought the opportunity of jobs and financial independence for young women. They became secretaries and telephonists in the new skyscraper office buildings.

To reflect their independence women began to wear shorter skirts. They also engaged in pastimes usually associated with men. Driving motorcycles and cars, flying aeroplanes and smoking cigarettes became female activities.

Young women who had jobs, wore short skirts and enjoyed parties and dancing were called flappers (see Source 2).

HOW DID POPULAR MUSIC AND DANCE CHANGE?

The 1920s became known as the Jazz Age. This form of music came from African-American blues music. Although it began as black music, it became very popular with whites as well. Instruments like the saxophone and trumpet formed the basis of jazz bands. Louis Armstrong, an African-American trumpet player, was one of the most popular entertainers of the decade (see biography).

Along with new music came new dances. Out went slow, sedate dances like the Waltz. In came more lively dances such as the Charleston and the Black Bottom.

The change in popular music styles was so great that large numbers of Americans took a dislike to jazz. Some white Americans even called it the 'devil's music' because they associated it with African-Americans.

LOUIS 'SATCHMO' ARMSTRONG (1901-1971)

Born in New Orleans, Armstrong was from a very poor family and learnt to play the cornet at reform school. He moved to Chicago in 1922, making his name as a brilliant jazz trumpeter. He later returned to New Orleans to a hero's welcome. Armstrong made his first records in 1925. He toured Europe throughout the 1930s with his own orchestra.

In 1947 he formed the Louis Armstrong Allstars and toured worldwide until the end of his life. This earned him immense popularity, respect and the nickname 'Ambassador Satch'.

Questions

1. Study Source 1. Even though the main characters of these films are different, why do you think they were both popular in the 1920s?
2. Study Source 2. Why do you think the actions of the flappers in the second photograph caused such a public stir in the 1920s?
3. Why was jazz frowned upon by many Americans in the 1920s?
4. What do you regard as the most important social change in America in the 1920s? Give reasons for your answer.

'The Roaring Twenties'

In a GCSE Modern World History examination candidates are asked several types of questions. These include:
• The evaluation of sources
• The evaluation of sources using your own knowledge
• Writing extended answers using your own knowledge

A fourth type is the structured question. In this type of question candidates are asked to use only their own knowledge to write an answer. The answers are similar to extended writing answers but tend to be shorter.

QUESTIONS AND GLORIA'S ANSWERS

(a) What were the main features of 'The Roaring Twenties'?

(4 marks)

> The 1920s were a period of great change in the USA. The country had an economic boom. This led to many Americans becoming rich. They had the chance to buy new products such as cars and radios. It was very different from the 1930s when the USA had an economic depression.

(b) Explain why prohibition was introduced.

(6 marks)

> Prohibition was where the USA banned the sale and drinking of alcohol. It was introduced by the 18th Amendment of the Constitution.
>
> Lots of people disliked alcoholic drinks. Many of these people were religious. The Women's Christian Temperance Union (WCTU) believed drink caused social problems. It ruined family life. Men would drink away their wages, leaving little money to bring up children. It also led to family problems. Wives were beaten up by drunken husbands.
>
> Alcohol drinking also created alcoholics. These were people who were addicted to drink. They sometimes became tramps and beggars.
>
> The WCTU spent years campaigning to get rid of alcohol drinking. Before 1918 many states had already got rid of alcohol drinking. They had introduced their own prohibition. By 1918 over three quarters of the states had introduced prohibition. In 1918 it was inevitable that all the USA would accept the idea.
>
> That is why prohibition was introduced.

(c) 'The most serious problem faced by American society during the 1920s was the poor treatment of black people.'
Do you agree with this statement? Explain your answer.

(10 marks)

> In the 1920s the USA faced many problems. In the big cities gangsters caused a big rise in crime. These gangsters made money from selling illegal 'booze' during prohibition. To make sure they could do this, they bribed the police and politicians. The most famous gangster was Al Capone. He was an Italian American and lived in Chicago. He ran illegal gambling, prostitution and drink rackets. To keep control of his operation, he murdered opponents. On St Valentine's Day, 1929, he had his enemies killed in the St Valentine's Day Massacre.
>
> The USA also had problems affecting black people. Many black people lived in the southern USA. They lived in poverty, producing cotton and tobacco. Many were sharecroppers. This meant they had to give a share of their crop to a landowner. These sharecroppers lived in absolute poverty. Many could not read or write.
>
> Black people also suffered from discrimination. In the southern states blacks faced segregation. This meant that they had to go to separate schools and live in different areas from whites.
>
> What made matters worse was the Ku Klux Klan. This was an organisation of white people. They disliked blacks, Catholics and Jews. They wanted white supremacy. They terrorised black people. Now and again black people were hanged without trial. This was lynching.

Therefore, black people were very badly treated. I think they had the worst problems, certainly worse than gangsters. In the 1930s, when prohibition ended, gangsters disappeared, but black people still suffered from discrimination.

HOW TO SCORE FULL MARKS – WHAT THE EXAMINERS SAY

Question (a)
Candidates are expected to identify those features of the 1920s that made the period 'The Roaring Twenties'.

Gloria mentions the production of more cars and the economic boom – both big factors in the 'Roaring Twenties'. However, they are only two factors. She could have mentioned the introduction of prohibition and the problems it caused. These included the growth of illegal drinking in 'speakeasies'. She could also have mentioned the development of organised crime, which was associated with breaking prohibition. In addition, she could have mentioned the growth of racism. This appeared with the rise of the Ku Klux Klan and the introduction of quotas in immigration.

As a result, Gloria received only 1 out of a possible 4 marks.

Question (b)
Candidates are expected to provide reasons for the introduction of prohibition. Marks will be given where **links** are made between reasons.

Gloria mentions two very important reasons for the introduction of prohibition. These are religious and moral reasons. She links these to the work of the Women's Christian Temperance Union. However, she could also have mentioned the work of the Anti-Saloon League (see p26).

In fact, Gloria misses a number of important points. 1918 saw the end of the First World War. There is a link between the war and the introduction of prohibition. During the war it was seen as unpatriotic to use grain to make alcohol because grain could also be used to feed US citizens and troops. So drinking alcohol became unpatriotic. Moreover, the war created a lot of anti-German feeling in the USA. German immigrants had created and owned most of the big breweries. These included Budweiser, Pabst and Schlitz. Therefore, getting rid of alcohol was seen as patriotic.

Gloria makes some good points but misses others. As a result, she received 3 out of a possible 6 marks.

Question (c)
This question requires candidates to engage in some extended writing to explain whether our not the poor treatment of black people was the most serious problem.

Gloria clearly identifies two major problems: organised crime and the poor treatment of black people. She explains why both of these problems are serious. She also explains why she thinks the treatment of black people is more serious than organised crime by stating that blacks still suffered discrimination beyond the 1920s, whereas other problems did not continue.

Gloria could have mentioned other problems. Many farmers, for example, suffered severe financial hardship in the 1920s. Also, the USA was a rapidly changing society in the 1920s due to the economic boom in industry. These rapid changes led to a growing intolerance. This intolerance was shown not only against black people but against foreign immigrants and people with left wing political views, like communists and socialists.

*Overall, Gloria explains some of the problems in 1920s America and **prioritises** them by stating that the poor treatment of black people was the most serious. But she does not mention all the problems that were apparent.*

As a result, she just missed out on top marks and received 8 out of a possible 10 marks.

EXTENSION WORK

'The Roaring Twenties' – is this a good description of the USA in the 1920s? Explain your answer, **using information and sources from the last two chapters and your own knowledge**.

(15 marks)

• OCR accepts no responsibility whatsoever for the accuracy or method of working in the answers given.

1920s: Prohibition and Prosperity

SOURCE A
Why prohibition was introduced in the USA.

During the First World War the supporters of prohibition took the chance to argue that it went against the USA to drink alcohol. This was apparently because it was often sold by Americans who had German backgrounds.

From a textbook written for use in British schools, published in 1981.

SOURCE B
Other reasons behind the introduction of prohibition.

The main base for the prohibition ideas came from the Methodist and Baptist Churches, or white southerners frightened of drunken blacks, or employers who wanted sober workers. They played on people's fear – of God or of fights between different races. Prohibition was intended to help gain the protection of God and Country..

From a book on 1920s America by an American historian, published in 1972.

QUESTIONS AND ANISH'S ANSWERS

(a) Do **Sources A** and **B** agree about the reasons for the introduction of prohibition?
Explain your answer using **Sources A** and **B**.
(AQA 2003)   *(5 marks)*

> Source A says that prohibition was introduced because of the war. The people who mainly sold alcohol drinks were Germans. The USA was on the Allied side and was opposed to Germany.
>
> Source B gives different reasons for the introduction of prohibition. It mentions religious reasons. Methodist and Baptist churches said that drinking alcohol was against God. Other people also wanted to see prohibition. Southern whites were frightened of drunken blacks so wanted it for racist reasons and employers wanted sober and not drunken workers.
>
> Therefore, Sources A and B offer different reasons for the introduction of prohibition.

(b) Is **Source A** more useful than **Source B** for studying the reasons for the introduction of prohibition?
Explain your answer using **Sources A** and **B** and your own knowledge.
(AQA 2003)   *(9 marks)*

> I do not think Source A is more useful than Source B for studying the reasons for the introduction of prohibition. Source B contains more reasons for the introduction of prohibition than Source A. Source A mentions one reason, the war. Source B mentions three reasons, religion, racism and the support of employers. Both sources are secondary sources so there is no real difference in their use, although Source B is written by an American historian, which makes it more useful.

SOURCE C

From a textbook written for British schools, published in 1964.

(c) **Source C** is a drawing from a school textbook. How accurate a representation do you think it is? Explain your answer using **Source C** and your own knowledge.
(AQA 2003)   *(10 marks)*

> Source C shows a raid on a speakeasy. A speakeasy was an illegal place to drink during prohibition. It shows men throwing bottles of alcohol at a wall. This was done to destroy the stock of alcoholic drink.
>
> I have actually seen a video of police doing just this sort of thing. So it must be accurate. Across America during the 1920s police raided speakeasies. When they found alcoholic drink there destroyed it. Sometimes they had their actions filmed. This was a way of showing that they were taking prohibition seriously.
>
> However, the source is a drawing. It is not a photograph. So the person producing the drawing might have changed things, which would affect its accuracy.

Question (a)

This question tests a candidate's ability to detect similarities and differences between sources.

To achieve full marks, candidates must find similarities as well as differences between the sources.

Anish mentions several differences between the sources: the issue of war in Source A and the religious, racial and business reasons of Source B. However, he doesn't identify similarities. The similarity between the sources concerns patriotism. Source A says prohibition was supported because it was seen as anti-German at a time of war with Germany. Source B refers to the need to gain the protection of 'God and Country'. They both suggest that prohibition was a patriotic duty.

As a result, Anish received 4 out of a possible 5 marks. If he had mentioned more data from the source he would have received full marks.

Question (b)

This question tests a candidate's ability to identify the usefulness of a source in the context of the introduction of prohibition.

To achieve full marks, candidates must mention both the strengths (usefulness) and the limitations of the sources. Candidates must also use their own knowledge to support their views.

Anish mentions the limitations and strengths of both sources in terms of numbers of reasons given. However, the reference to the fact that both are secondary sources and that one of the sources is written by an American historian do not really address the question properly.

There is no evidence that he has used his own knowledge. Anish could have mentioned that prohibition was introduced towards the end of the First World War, and that the immediate cause of prohibition was the war. Therefore, this might make Source A more useful. Conversely, Anish could have mentioned that groups such as the Women's Christian Temperance Union and the Anti-Saloon League put forward strong religious and moral reasons for the introduction of prohibition.

As a result, because Anish did not directly refer to his own knowledge to support his argument, he received 5 out of a possible 9 marks.

Question (c)

This question tests a candidate's ability to analyse and evaluate the drawing in **Source 3** in the context of prohibition.

To achieve full marks candidates would be expected to refer to where the source comes from, or who produced it, and why. **Source 3** has been produced for a British school textbook. It is therefore likely to be accurate because the author plans to explain to students what actually happened in the USA during prohibition.

Candidates should also use their own knowledge to explain how accurate the drawing is, based on historical fact.

Anish's answer contains a very good explanation of the potential accuracy of the drawing using his own knowledge. He assesses the accuracy in relation to information he has acquired during the GCSE course.

He also makes a reference to the possibility of inaccuracy because it is a drawing and not a photograph, although this contradicts his earlier statement.

As a result, Anish received 8 out of a possible 10 marks.

EXTENSION WORK

What were the main reasons behind the introduction of prohibition in 1920? How far was it effective? Explain your answer, **using information and sources from the last two chapters and your own knowledge.**

(15 marks)

• AQA accepts no responsibility whatsoever for the accuracy or method of working in the answers given.

Boom turns to bust – causes of the Depression

To many Americans the boom years of the 1920s would never end. Each year share prices rose and the size of the economy grew. However, even before the collapse of the New York Stock Market on Wall Street in October 1929, the signs of an economic depression were present.

UNEQUAL DISTRIBUTION OF WEALTH

Although the economy grew rapidly during the 1920s, not everyone benefited. In a survey produced in 1928, 60 per cent of families were earning under $2,000 per year. In contrast, the top five per cent of the population owned 33 per cent of the country's wealth. The groups who missed out on the new economic wealth were farmers, African-Americans and workers in industries like coalmining.

Because the economy was based on low wage earners, it lacked the demand to buy the large number of goods being produced.

OVERPRODUCTION

The mass production techniques of Henry Ford and other businessmen meant that large numbers of goods could be produced (see p22). The problem for the US economy was that not enough people were rich enough to buy them. By 1928 some companies had begun to cut down on production. To achieve this aim, they laid off workers. Unemployment began to rise. This began a process that led to ever-increasing falls in consumer demand. The more unemployed people there were, the less consumer demand there was. This laid the foundations for the economic depression.

> **SOURCE 1**
> 'The most serious weakness of the economy was that the capacity to produce had outrun the capacity to consume. The mass of people, though better off than before, were unable to buy their share of consumer goods and support the level of mass production.'
>
> **Adapted from** *The Limits of Liberty*, **by British historian MA Jones, 1983.**

THE INTERNATIONAL ECONOMIC SITUATION

Although demand was limited at home, it was possible for US companies to sell goods abroad. However, the introduction of the Fordney-McCumber tariff in 1922 reduced international trade. This tariff taxed imported goods, so that home produced goods would appear cheaper than foreign goods. It was introduced in order to encourage Americans to buy American goods. In 1930 the Hawley-Smoot tariff put even higher taxes on imported goods. This led to a fall in international trading and made the depression worse.

Also, economies in European countries like Germany had not recovered fully from the First World War. In Latin America and the Far East political instability worsened the situation.

> **SOURCE 2**
> *"During the past twelve months we have suffered with other nations from economic depression. Worldwide causes – overproduction of certain goods abroad, financial crises in many countries, political trouble in Asia, revolutions in South America – have all contributed to causing the depression."*
>
> **From a speech by President Herbert Hoover, December 2, 1930.**

GOVERNMENT POLICY

The laissez-faire policy of the government made matters worse. The lack of government controls on buying shares led to excessive **share speculation**. This process pushed the value of companies high above their true value. When a downturn occurred in the Stock Market in October 1929, investors panicked.

> **share speculation**
> *buying shares with the aim of selling them quickly for profit*

WEAKNESS OF THE BANKING SYSTEM

Nationwide Fever of Stock Speculation!

Eager buying has reached all classes of people throughout the country and has set new records in many directions.

Unlike other major economies, the USA lacked nationwide banks. Instead it had thousands of small banks. None of these banks had sufficient cash reserves to survive a downturn in the economy. Even during the boom years, banks suffered failure. Between 1921 and 1928 5,000 banks failed. In 1929, even before the Wall Street Crash, 659 banks closed.

As ordinary Americans built up large debts through hire purchase, an economic depression was just around the corner.

Crowds on Wall Street, where speculation on the stock market had made many Americans rich.

DID THE WALL STREET CRASH CAUSE THE DEPRESSION?

When the New York Stock Market faced a major sale of shares in October 1929 it merely showed up weaknesses already existing in the economy. The Wall Street Crash did not cause the economic depression, it was merely the start of it.

Questions

1. Study Sources 1 and 2.
   a) In what ways do they differ in their explanation of why the economic depression began?
   b) Why do you think these two sources offer different interpretations of the causes of depression?
2. How did activities like the one mentioned in Source 3 make the US economy unstable in the 1920s?
3. Study the causes of the economic depression mentioned above. Place the reasons in order of importance. Give reasons for your choice.

The Wall Street Crash

THE DAY THAT SHOOK THE WORLD

Wall Street on the island of Manhattan in New York City is the home of the New York Stock Exchange. Here companies across America put up their shares or stock for sale. In the 1920s the value of companies was measured by the value of their stock. Although other stock exchanges existed across the country, Wall Street was by far the largest.

Black Thursday
On the morning of Thursday, October 24 (which became known as Black Thursday), the buying and selling of shares began as normal. However, in a short time it became clear that most people wanted to sell their shares. By the time trading closed nearly 13 million shares had changed hands. Most of the shares were sold. Hardly any were bought.

In one day the American economy was in ruins. The value of companies fell alarmingly. Millions of dollars were lost by share investors. So strong was the panic that some investors committed suicide by throwing themselves from skyscrapers.

By evening on Black Thursday, the Chicago, Illinois, and Buffalo (up-state New York) stock exchanges had also suffered huge losses. They closed their doors to further trading.

Black Tuesday
The next Monday, October 28, share prices dropped again. Nine million shares were sold. On the following day, October 29 – Black Tuesday – the stock market faced almost complete collapse. 16,383,700 shares changed hands, many for next to nothing. The losses in value on that day were $10 billion. Prices continued to fall until 1932!

SOURCE 1

Share prices of US companies before and after the Wall Street Crash.

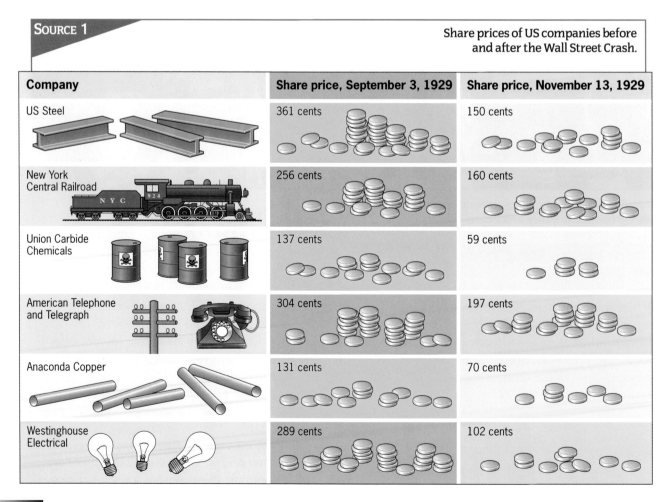

Company	Share price, September 3, 1929	Share price, November 13, 1929
US Steel	361 cents	150 cents
New York Central Railroad	256 cents	160 cents
Union Carbide Chemicals	137 cents	59 cents
American Telephone and Telegraph	304 cents	197 cents
Anaconda Copper	131 cents	70 cents
Westinghouse Electrical	289 cents	102 cents

Share speculation

A major cause of the collapse was share speculation. During the 1920s the Stock Market rose steadily in value. This is called a Bull Market. It seemed that prices could never fall. So many people were making fortunes on the stock exchange that ordinary people not usually interested in buying shares began to take part.

To buy a share all you had to do was pay a deposit of ten per cent of the share's value and pay the remainder later. As share prices always seemed to go up you couldn't lose. This practice was called buying on the margin. Even though buyers may not have had the money to pay the full price of the share, it didn't matter. Everyone seemed to be making money.

As people were buying shares merely to sell on at a profit, it led to the over-valuation of companies (the prices people paid for shares were often too high). Once share prices began to fall, a panic set in. People rushed to sell their shares before they lost money. The Bull Market of the 1920s was replaced by the Bear Market of the early 1930s, a period of falling prices. People had short memories: a similar boom had taken place in land prices in Florida in the early 1920s. In 1926 the market collapsed suddenly, leaving thousands of people ruined.

SOURCE 2	By a financial journalist from the New York Herald Tribune newspaper, October 22, 1929.

'I believe that in the last few days we have driven down stocks to hard rock [the lowest price]. I believe we will have a ragged market for a few weeks and then the beginning of a stock rise that will gain momentum next year.'

A wealthy New Yorker shortly after the Wall Street Crash.

British interest rates

Another cause was the decision by the Bank of England in mid-October 1929 to raise British interest rates to 6.5 per cent. Interest rates represent the amount a bank will pay a customer for placing their money with the bank. If the interest rate is five per cent and a person leaves £100 in an account for a year, he or she will have £105 pounds in their account at the end of the year. If a bank or country raises its interest rate, it would attract people from other banks or countries wishing to get more for their money. The aim was to attract money back to Britain that had been spent on buying US shares. This led to a fall in share prices. This helps explain why shareholders wanted to sell at that time.

Questions

1. Study Source 1.
   a) Which company suffered the greatest fall in value from the information contained in this source?
   b) What is the overall percentage drop in share prices?
2. Study Source 2.
   a) How useful is this source as evidence of opinion about the New York Stock Market in October 1929? Explain your answer.
   b) Explain why a newspaper like the Herald Tribune was so mistaken about the condition of the stock market. Give reasons for your answer.
3. How did 'buying on the margin' create the conditions for a major stock market collapse in October 1929?

AMERICA IN ECONOMIC CRISIS

The Wall Street Crash of October 1929 began the worst economic depression in the history of the world. As the world's richest and largest economy, the USA suffered severely. The **Gross National Product** of the USA was $104 billion in 1929. It had fallen to $59 billion by 1932. From October 1929 economic production dropped rapidly as hundreds of factories closed. Hundreds of thousands became unemployed. This caused a downward spiral or vicious circle in the economy, which created even greater hardship (see Source 2).

> **Gross National Product**
> *the total amount of goods and services produced by an economy annually*

SOURCE 1		Unemployment in the USA, 1929 to 1933.

YEAR	Millions unemployed	Percentage of workforce unemployed
1929	1.6	2.3%
1930	4.3	8.7%
1931	8.0	15.9%
1932	12.1	23.6%
1933	14.0	24.9%

SOURCE 2

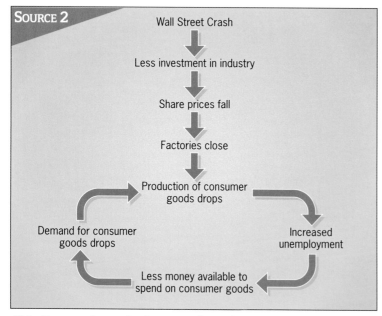

This diagram shows the downward spiral or vicious circle of the USA's economic crisis.

Unfortunately, very few states had any sort of welfare programme to help those out of work. In 1930 Frank Murphy, Mayor of Detroit, Michigan, told President Hoover that people in his city were on the edge of starvation. Yet the federal government did not intervene to help the unemployed directly until July 1932.

SOURCE 3

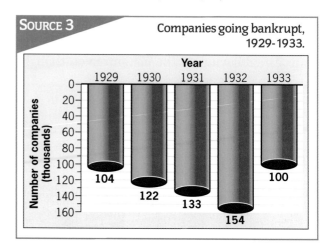

Companies going bankrupt, 1929-1933.

THE DISINTEGRATION OF HOME AND FAMILY

Without work and government support thousands lost their homes because they couldn't keep up their loan repayments. **Shanty towns** grew up around virtually every town and city. These were called Hoovervilles after President Hoover, whom many blamed for their appalling situation. Others crossed the country by jumping on goods trains in search of work. These homeless people (known as hobos) faced both hardship and attacks from armed groups employed by railroads to stop them using free rail travel. To get food, the homeless and unemployed had to rely on charity. They joined breadlines for free soup and bread, and paid what they could to sleep sitting upright, on chairs, in a room alongside hundreds of others.

> **shanty towns**
> *housing created by the homeless, made from whatever materials could be found*

A Hooverville in Seattle, Washington during the Depression.

SOURCE 5

A job agency during the Depression.

Poor diet and a feeling of hopelessness increased ill health. The suicide rate increased and family break-ups became common amongst the unemployed. By 1933, over 300,000 children no longer attended school.

| SOURCE 6 | From an interview with Peggy Terry of Kentucky. She describes a Hooverville outside Oklahoma City. |

"The Hooverville was the most incredible thing. Here people were living in old, rusted car bodies. That was their home. There were people living in shacks made of orange crates. One family with a whole lot of kids were living in a piano box. This wasn't just a little section, this was maybe ten miles wide and ten miles long. People living in whatever they could junk together."

Questions

1. Study Sources 1, 2, and 3.
   Explain how the Wall Street Crash helped cause the United States economy to go into a depression.

2. Study Sources 4 and 5.
   Do you think these photographs fully explain the impact of the Depression on the USA between 1929 and 1933? Explain your answer.

3. Study Source 6.
   How useful is an interview with an eyewitness like Peggy Terry to an historian writing about the impact of the Depression on the USA?

4. 'Without Government help the USA could not get out of economic depression.'
   Using information in this section, explain how this view helps us understand why the economic depression was so severe in the USA between 1929 and 1933.

President Hoover – villain or scapegoat?

When Americans of the time were asked what they most closely associated with President Hoover, the majority answered "economic depression". To many he was to blame for all the unemployment and misery associated with the period 1929 to 1932.

In the 1980s an American film called *Annie* was released. It was set in New York City in 1932, at the height of the Depression. In it, a group of homeless people sing a song to Hoover (see Source 1).

bureaucrat
someone overly dedicated to complex and slow official procedures

But, in reality, does Hoover deserve all of the blame?

THE CASE AGAINST HOOVER

Economic policies
Before he became President, Hoover had been a leading member of the Republican governments of the 1920s. As Secretary for Commerce, he had been directly responsible for many Republican economic policies. These policies helped cause the Wall Street Crash of October 1929 (see p36) and the economic depression that followed.

In the 1928 presidential election campaign Hoover claimed: "We in America are nearer to the final triumph over poverty than ever before in the history of any land." Yet within 18 months hundreds of thousands of Americans had lost their jobs and the economy was in crisis.

Shifting responsibility
Hoover believed in a laissez-faire economic policy, suggesting that the government should play as small a role as possible in economic matters. Even when factories closed and unemployment rose, Hoover seemed to do virtually nothing. Instead, he kept claiming that "prosperity was just around the corner". To Hoover, businessmen had created the Depression. It was their job to get America out of it.

Children in a Hooverville, July 1932. What does this photograph suggest about the popularity of Hoover?

HERBERT HOOVER (1874-1964)

The 31st President of the USA, Hoover was born in West Branch, Iowa, and educated at Stanford University in California. After qualifying as an engineer, from 1919 to 1921 he was involved in organising relief to help those affected by the First World War. He was Secretary for Commerce from 1921 to 1928, and his presidency (1929-1933) followed.

He thought the main cause of economic depression lay outside the USA: only when world trade increased could depression end. However, to protect the American economy from foreign competition, Hoover introduced the Hawley-Smoot Tariff in 1930 (see p36). This increased import duties on foreign goods entering the US economy. It made matters worse by slowing down world trade.

Hoover also believed in 'rugged individualism'. To him, Americans should not rely on government help. They should work hard by themselves to end the Depression. He also believed in 'voluntaryism'. This meant that charities and private citizens should help the unemployed and poor, not the government.

So, as unemployment reached nearly 12 million in the spring of 1932, Hoover was seen by many as a helpless, hopeless President incapable of dealing with the economic crisis.

THE CASE FOR HERBERT HOOVER

Factors beyond presidential control

President Hoover faced the worst economic crisis in American history. Almost the entire world economy had collapsed along with that of the USA.

Moreover, Hoover was limited in what he could do to remedy the situation by the system of government in the USA. Responsibility for helping the unemployed and poor lay with the states, not the federal government (see p8). Also, to pass laws, Hoover needed the support of the national parliament – Congress. Without support from state governments and Congress, Hoover could achieve little on his own. In fact, Hoover did not receive much support because members of Congress did not want to raise taxes to help pay for the unemployed.

International and federal aid

However, Hoover did try to help. During the First World War the USA had lent millions of dollars to Britain, France and Belgium. They borrowed US money to buy armaments and were expected to pay it back at the end of the war. Hoover cancelled these debts in 1931. This aimed to increase world trade by leaving Britain, France and Belgium with more money to buy goods.

Hoover also introduced the first direct aid by the federal government. In January 1932 the

SOURCE 2

How have historians judged Herbert Hoover?

'Hoover, white-faced, exhausted, stumbling in speech, swayed on the election platform. After the speech a Republican said, "Why don't they make him quit? He's not doing himself or the party any good. It's turning into a farce. He is tired physically and mentally"'.

Adapted from *The Crisis of the Old Order*, by American historian Arthur Schlesinger, 1957. He is writing about the 1932 presidential election campaign.

'During his presidential term Hoover was to act incessantly, doing more than any previous President had done in any previous economic crisis.'

Adapted from *The Longman History of the United States*, by British historian Hugh Brogan, 1999.

Reconstruction Finance Corporation (RFC) was created. It gave $2 billion to help banks and businesses. When FDR became President in March 1933, he kept the RFC as an important part of his own policies.

In July 1932 the Emergency Relief and Construction Act was passed. This gave direct federal aid to the unemployed. In the same month federal home loans were given to people who had difficulty paying off their **mortgages**.

mortgage
a loan to buy a house

> **!** INVESTIGATE...
> *What else did Hoover do to try to lift the USA out of the Depression? Visit* www.hoover.arc hives.gov/index.html. *and click on 'Virtual Exhibits'.*

Questions

1. Study Source 1. How useful is the song to an historian studying public opinion of Hoover in the early 1930s?
2. Study Source 2.
   a) In what ways are the two historians' views different?
   b) Why do you think they are different? Give reasons for your answer.

Democrat landslide! The 1932 elections

AMERICA SWITCHES SIDES

The 1932 elections were a turning point in American history. In the period 1920 to 1932 the Republican Party controlled the government. It also controlled Congress for most of that period. Many of the 48 state governments were also Republican.

The 1932 elections changed all that. The Democratic Party won the presidential election. It also won majorities in both the Senate and House of Representatives (see p9). Across the United States, Democrats controlled **state legislatures** and **governorships**.

From 1933 to 1953 the Democrats controlled the presidency and government. They dominated the Senate and House of Representatives for most of the 1933-1981 period. Why did such a major change take place?

state legislatures *parliaments in each of the 48 states*

state governorship *state equivalent of the President*

SOURCE 1		The 1932 presidential election result.
	Popular Votes	Electoral College Votes
F.D. Roosevelt (Democrat)	22,829,501	472
H. Hoover (Republican)	15,760,684	59

HERBERT HOOVER'S FAILURE TO END THE DEPRESSION

The main reason for Republican defeat was the economic depression. From October 1929 to 1932 unemployment rose steadily. Millions lost their jobs. Factories and banks closed in their thousands. Faced with such an economic catastrophe, the President seemed incapable of bringing back economic prosperity. Hoover's claim in the 1928 election that he would provide America with "a chicken in every pot and a car in every garage" looked ridiculous by 1932.

The Republican hope that the economy would 'right itself' without extensive government intervention had not worked. Hoover took most of the blame. He became a figure of fun. The shanty towns of the homeless were called 'Hoovervilles'. The newspapers used by the homeless to cover themselves at night were called 'Hoover blankets'. In 1932 hitch-hikers carried signs reading, 'If you don't give me a lift, I'll vote for Hoover'!

THE BONUS ARMY EPISODE OF 1932

To make matters worse the Government received very poor publicity in Hoover's handling of the 'Bonus Army'. Soldiers who had fought in the First World War were due to receive pensions in 1945. However, due to the Depression, thousands marched on Washington DC in 1932 demanding their war bonus immediately. A shanty town of protestors was created near the centre of Washington DC at Anacostia Flats. The Congress refused to give the bonus. On July 28, 1932, at the height of the election campaign, US troops under the command of General Douglas MacArthur forcibly removed the protestors. Two protestors were killed and several hundred were wounded. This incident made President Hoover look like an insensitive and cruel man

FRANKLIN D ROOSEVELT (1882-1945)
FDR was born in Hyde Park, New York State and educated at Harvard University and Columbia Law School. The 32nd President of the USA, he was also cousin of the 26th President, Theodore Roosevelt (1901-1909). After training as a lawyer, he became Assistant Secretary to the Navy from 1913 to 1921, and vice-Presidential candidate for the Democrats in 1920. He was then elected governor of New York State (1930-1932), and went on to become the only person in US history to win four Presidential elections: 1932, 1936, 1940, 1944. He died in Office.

WHO VOTED FOR FDR?

The Democratic Party candidate, Franklin D Roosevelt, organised a very effective campaign. This was despite being crippled by polio and being unable to walk unaided. From his previous positions of office (see biography) he had a record of effective aid to the poor, unemployed and homeless in his own state. A powerful speaker, during his campaign he called for a "New Deal for the American people" to end the Depression. Without mentioning any specific reforms, he said he would support "bold experimentation" to deal with America's economic problems.

SOURCE 2

He won support from trade unionists across America. He also won support from traditional Democrat voters such as whites in the Old South, and immigrant groups like Jewish, Irish and Italian Americans. Above all, he seemed to offer the only way forward for the USA to get out of economic depression. Many US voters had simply lost faith in Hoover and the Republicans.

FDR won a sweeping victory and the Democrats also won overall control of both houses of Congress. When he became President in March 1933, FDR would have widespread support to get reform through Congress to end the Depression.

SOURCE 3 | Adapted from a biography of FDR, by Ted Morgan, 1985.

'FDR won because he was not Herbert Hoover.'

THE 'LAME DUCK' MONTHS, NOVEMBER 1932 – MARCH 1933

Although he won the election in the first Tuesday in November, FDR had to wait until March 1933 to actually become President. This period was contained in the US Constitution. It was meant to give the incoming President time to form a government. The period from November 1932 to March 1933 was known as the 'Lame Duck' period because Hoover was still in office but lacked any real authority to introduce major reform.

In the circumstances of 1932 to 1933, the delay in forming a new government only made matters worse. Hoover offered to work with FDR to bring relief to the unemployed but FDR refused to co-operate. At no time during the 'Lame Duck' period did FDR tell the American public what he was going to do. By the time he became President, all the banks across America were closed and 25 per cent of the work force were unemployed.

Cartoon of March 3, 1933. It shows FDR throwing out the policies of the previous Republican government. Herbert Hoover is on the right.

Questions

1. Study Source 1. Use information from pages 8-9 to explain why there is such a difference between FDR's margin of victory in popular votes compared to the margin of victory in electoral college votes.
2. Study Source 2.
   a) What are the Republican policies FDR in throwing away in the dustbin?
   b) Why do you think these policies failed to get America out of the economic depression?
   c) How useful is this cartoon as evidence of why FDR won the 1932 presidential election?
3. Using information in this chapter, would you agree that the economic depression was the only reason behind FDR's victory in the 1932 Presidential election? Explain your answer.

Hoover and the 1932 election

A photograph of a shanty town in Seattle, taken in 1931

SOURCE C   An election poster of 1932

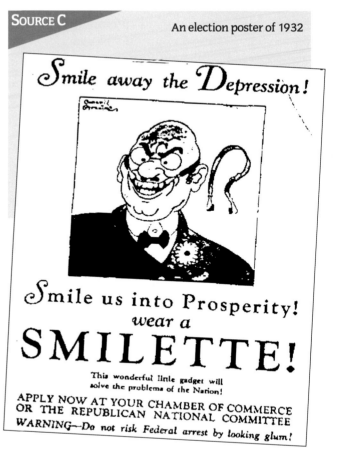

Smile away the Depression!

Smile us into Prosperity!
wear a
SMILETTE!
This wonderful little gadget will solve the problems of the Nation!
APPLY NOW AT YOUR CHAMBER OF COMMERCE OR THE REPUBLICAN NATIONAL COMMITTEE
WARNING—Do not risk Federal arrest by looking glum!

SOURCE B   "Millions of our citizens cherish the hope that their old standards of living have not gone forever. Those millions shall not hope in vain. I pledge you, I pledge myself, to a New Deal for the American people. This is more than a political campaign; it is a call to arms. Give me your help, not to win votes alone, but to win this crusade to restore America… I am waging a war against Destruction, Delay, Deceit and Despair…"

A pre-election speech given by Roosevelt, 1932.

QUESTIONS AND SAM'S ANSWERS

(a) Study **Source A**.
Do you think this photograph would help Hoover's election campaign of 1932?
Use the Source and your knowledge to explain your answer.

(7 marks)

Source A is a photograph of an American shanty town in 1931. These shanty towns were called Hoovervilles. They were created by the unemployed and homeless during the Depression. Hoover was President during the Depression. His political party, the Republicans, were seen as responsible for all the unemployment and poverty caused by the Depression. After the Wall Street Crash of October 1929, Hoover and his government did little to help the unemployed. In contrast, the Democrat candidate, Franklin Roosevelt, did offer hope. He offered a New Deal for the American people. He promised to get America back to work. So this photograph would not help Hoover, it would help Franklin Roosevelt in his election to be President in 1932.

(b) Study **Source B**.
Do you think this was an effective campaign speech?
Use the Source and your knowledge to explain your answer.

(7 marks)

I think this is a very good campaign speech. FDR tells the American people how bad the Depression really is. He also tells the American people that he will offer them a New Deal, which will get them back to work. FDR also asks the American people to join him in a crusade against the Depression. He wants the people's support. This makes it an effective campaign speech.

(c) Study **Source C**.
Do you think this poster was published by the Democrats or the Republicans?
Use the Source and your knowledge to explain your answer.

(7 marks)

I think the campaign poster came from the Democrat Party. This was the party of FDR. It says 'Smile away the Depression!' This is making fun of the policies of President Hoover, a Republican. People in America thought Hoover had not really done much to deal with the Depression. It also says at the bottom of the poster 'Apply now at your Chamber of Commerce or the Republican National Committee'. This is an attempt to give the idea that it was a Republican poster. The Democrats had accused Hoover of doing nothing to end the Depression. This poster is a way of showing what they meant in an amusing way. That is why this is a Democrat poster not a Republican poster, even though it mentions the Republican Party at the bottom of the poster.

HOW TO SCORE FULL MARKS – WHAT THE EXAMINERS SAY

Question (a)

This question requires a candidate to comprehend a source as well as use their own knowledge to explain how that source is linked to the presidential election campaign of 1932. There are 3 marks for using your own knowledge and 4 marks for comprehension of the source.

Sam provides a very full answer. He mentions the fact that shanty towns of the unemployed and homeless were called Hoovervilles after the President. He also mentions that many Americans believed Hoover had done virtually nothing to end the Depression. At the end of his answer Sam links this information to the question by stating that photographs like the one in Source A would not help Hoover's campaign. In a way, Sam produces rather too much information! Using information from Source B, he refers to FDR and the Democrat campaign for a New Deal. This is not required for this answer. Under examination conditions Sam would have spent precious time providing this extra information. This would have meant that he would have had less time to answer the other questions.

Nevertheless, this was a very good answer and received full marks, 7 out of 7.

Question (b)

Like **Question (a)**, this requires candidates to comprehend a source and use their own knowledge. This time 4 marks are available for the use of your own knowledge and 3 marks are available for comprehending the source.

Compared to Sam's first answer, this is rather short. Although he mentions some of the content of Source B, he doesn't relate it clearly to the idea of what an effective campaign speech is. FDR uses phrases like "a call to arms". This suggests that America is facing a crisis similar to a war. FDR also makes a direct promise to the American people: "I pledge you, I pledge myself, to a New Deal". Additionally, FDR closes his speech cleverly by using words which all begin with the same letter: "Destruction, Delay, Deceit and Despair". This is called alliteration and reinforces his point. Although Sam states that he thinks this is a good campaign speech, he does not link his comments directly with the content of the source or his own knowledge. He should also mention that this was a strong campaign speech compared to Hoover's speeches, which were regarded as dull and lacking hope for the future.

As a result, he received a mark out of 4 marks. To get full marks (out of 7) he should have made more reference to the text and his own knowledge of FDR's campaign.

Question (c)

This question requires candidates to understand the reasons behind producing a source. For that skill, the candidate could receive 4 marks. In addition, by including their own knowledge, a further 2 marks could be scored.

Sam rightly identifies that this is a comic and not a serious poster. Even though it states at the bottom of the poster that it was produced by the Republican National Committee, Sam still believes it was produced by the Democrats. Using his own knowledge he points out that the Democrats are FDR's party and that the Republicans are Hoover's party. He identifies a message in the poster. The message, according to Sam, is that Hoover and the Republicans had done virtually nothing to end the Depression.

For this answer Sam received 5 out of a possible 6 marks. If Sam had mentioned the lack of government action by Hoover with the idea that the Republicans were trying to smile their way out of the Depression, he would have received full marks.

EXTENSION WORK

What were the effects of the Depression on the American people? Explain your answer, **using sources and information in the last chapter and your own knowledge**.

(15 marks)

• OCR accepts no responsibility whatsoever for the accuracy or method of working in the answers given.

• OCR specimen question paper (2000) GCSE History B (Modern World).

The '100 Days', March to June 1933

WHAT WAS THE NEW DEAL?

The New Deal is the name given to the policies followed by the federal (national) and state governments to deal with the social and economic problems created by the Depression. It lasted from 1933 to 1941. It can be divided into three stages: the First New Deal (March 1933 to January 1935); the Second New Deal (January 1935 to January 1937); and the Third New Deal (1937 to 1941).

The President in this period was Franklin D Roosevelt, known as FDR. He was a Democrat and his election in November 1932 gave most Americans hope that the Depression would come to an end. In his Inauguration Address on March 4, 1933, he said: "This nation asks for action, and action now. Our greatest task is to put people to work. We must act, and act quickly. I shall ask the Congress for the one remaining instrument to meet the crisis – broad executive power to wage a war against the emergency as great as the power that would be given me if we were invaded by a foreign enemy."

FDR's 'New Deal' aimed to bring about Relief, Recovery and Reform in America. Relief for those who suffered poverty and unemployment. Recovery of the economy to bring an end to the Depression and Reform of the US economy so that a depression would not occur again.

SOURCE 1

A cartoon in an American newspaper, 1933. What statement is it trying to make?

WHAT ACTIONS DID FDR TAKE DURING THE '100 DAYS'?

In 1932, the Democrats not only won the presidential election but also gained majorities in both houses of Congress. In the first three months of office, FDR passed a variety of reforms dealing with the problems of the Depression years. FDR was the first President to speak directly to the American people about his plans for reform. He won support for them in a series of 'fireside chats' over the radio.

The banking crisis, 1933

The most serious problem facing the USA when FDR became President was the banking crisis. During the Depression several thousand small banks had collapsed. By early 1933, 4000 had closed down. When he became President on March 4, all banks across America had closed. FDR moved quickly to declare a national banking holiday from March 6 to 9. During this time, Congress passed the Emergency Banking Act. It aimed to restore confidence in the banking system. Only banks regarded as financially sound were allowed to reopen on March 9.

On June 16 the Glass-Steagall Banking Act became law. This act created the Federal Deposit Insurance Corporation (FDIC), which gave financial support to banks.

These two acts saved the banking system from collapse and laid the foundations for economic recovery.

Helping the Unemployed CCC

When FDR became President 12.8 million Americans were unemployed. This was 25 per cent of the workforce. At the end of March the Unemployment Relief Act created the first of the 'Alphabet Agencies', the Civilian Conservation Corps (CCC). It gave men aged 18 to 25 the opportunity to work. Under the direction of the army they could earn $30 a month, of which $25 went to their families. They lived in camps and helped

> **Alphabet Agencies** *name given to New Deal agencies such as the AAA, CCC, FERA, NRA, PWA and TVA*

develop National and State Parks, building roads and conservation projects. By August 1933, 250,000 worked for the CCC. It lasted until 1942.

FERA

In May the Federal Emergency Relief Administration (FERA) was created. It was under the control of Harry Hopkins (see p50). It aimed to help the unemployed by giving money to state governments. With a budget of $500 million it organised the construction of over 5,000 public buildings. However, the FERA also created **boondoggle jobs** just to give some form of employment. These types of jobs attracted criticism.

boondoggle jobs
jobs of virtually no economic value, created to give the unemployed work

PWA

In June, as part of the National Industrial Recovery Act, the Public Works Administration (PWA) was created. It was given $3.3 billion to help end the Depression. The PWA was under the control of Harold Ickes, Secretary of the Interior (see p51). He had a completely different view to Harry Hopkins about spending money. He refused to create boondoggle jobs. He wanted to use federal money wisely. Hopkins had spent $5 million to help the unemployed within two hours of taking office. In the first six months Ickes had spent only $110 million of his huge budget. Eventually the PWA built 50,000 miles of roads and 13,000 schools.

Helping Farmers

Under the leadership of Henry Wallace, the Agricultural Adjustment Administration (AAA) helped farmers (see p56). Farmers were also encouraged to destroy crops and livestock to help raise prices. This was seen as waste at a time of hunger and unemployment. However, it helped prevent farmers from going bust.

Reforming Business

In June 1933 the National Recovery Administration (NRA) was created under General Hugh Johnson (see p52). It aimed to end child labour and help workers get better conditions. It also helped trade unions bargain for better wages. The NRA was also given $3.3 billion to spend on helping businesses that

accepted its code of practice. Firms that did so could display a 'Blue Eagle' sign. To many the Blue Eagle became the symbol of the First New Deal. Not all industries benefited. It did not cover agricultural workers or domestic servants. It also encouraged price fixing, which worked in the favour of big companies.

Helping Poor Regions

In May 1933 the Tennessee Valley Authority (TVA) was created. It aimed to help the poor region known as the Upper South (see map). The TVA covered seven states and 55,000 sq km. It helped build dams to prevent flooding and produced electricity, helping local industry and farming. In 1933 only two per cent of farms in the region had electricity. By 1945 the figure had risen to 75 per cent. The TVA still exists today.

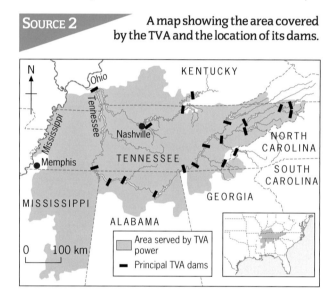

SOURCE 2 — A map showing the area covered by the TVA and the location of its dams.

Questions

1. *Describe the ways the government helped the unemployed during the '100 Days'.*
2. *In what ways were the '100 Days' a success in dealing with the problems created by the Depression?*
3. *In what ways could the '100 Days' be criticised? Explain your answer.*
4. *The New Deal hoped to bring Relief, Recovery and Reform. Construct a timeline. Next to each act of the '100 Days', write which ones tried to bring:*
   a) Relief to the unemployed
   b) Recovery to the economy
   c) Reform to prevent further depression.

The New Deal and unemployment

HOW DID FDR DECREASE UNEMPLOYMENT?

In his acceptance speech as President, FDR had said: "Our greatest primary task is to put people to work." When FDR became President in March 1933, 13 million (25 per cent of the workforce) were unemployed. Many had not only lost their jobs, but also their homes. Every night thousands of half-starved unemployed queued up at charity soup kitchens and slept in Hoovervilles.

New Deal measures introduced directly to help the unemployed

- Unemployed Relief Act created the Civilian Conservation Corps (CCC): March 1933
- Federal Emergency Relief Administration (FERA): May 1933
- National Industrial Recovery Act created the Public Works Administration (PWA): June 1933
- Civil Works Administration (CWA): November 1933
- Works Progress Administration (WPA): April 1935

FEDERAL RELIEF ADMINISTRATION (FERA), MARCH 1933

This Alphabet Agency aimed to give immediate help to the unemployed. FDR gave it a budget of $500 million. It did not give aid to unemployed people directly. Instead, it gave money to the states. This emphasised the federal nature of American government because, under the Constitution, the states had direct responsibility to aid the unemployed.

Harry Hopkins, a former social worker, was put in charge of this agency and, within two hours of taking up office, had spent $5 million on schemes to get the unemployed back to work. He wanted to give the unemployed jobs – any job – as soon as possible. This he believed would restore confidence in the country and give hope for the future. The FERA was criticised by its opponents for providing boondoogle jobs (see p42).

Hopkins also had problems persuading some reluctant state governments to use FERA money to help the unemployed. Nevertheless, by 1935 over $3 billion had been spent on aiding the unemployed, compared to 1932's figure of $208 million. The historian Tony Badger wrote that, 'Harry Hopkins's relief programmes were the key to the success of Roosevelt's short-term efforts to [end] distress.' In total, the FERA helped to construct:

- 5000 public buildings
- 7000 bridges

CIVIL WORKS ADMINISTRATION (CWA), NOVEMBER 1933 - MARCH 1934

For all Hopkins's efforts, unemployment still remained a major problem as the winter of 1933 to 1934 approached. As a result, FDR created another Alphabet Agency, the CWA, to offer emergency relief over the winter months. Harry Hopkins was again put in charge, with a budget of $400 million. Unlike the FERA, the CWA could intervene directly to aid the unemployed. Spending nearly $200 million a month to provide jobs for the poor and unemployed, the CWA lasted from November 1933 to March 1934.

HARRY HOPKINS (1890-1945)

Hopkins was a close adviser to FDR. He was head of FERA between 1933 and 1935. From 1933 to 1934 he also ran the Civil Works Administration (CWA), which gave emergency relief to the unemployed over the winter. From 1935 to 1938 he became head of the Works Progress Administration – the most important alphabet agency of the New Deal.

PUBLIC WORKS ADMINISTRATION (PWA), JUNE 1933

This Alphabet Agency was part of the National Industrial Recovery Act (NIRA). It was under the control of the Secretary of the Interior, Harold Ickes. Ickes had a very different approach to Harry Hopkins. He did not wish to create boondoggle jobs. He aimed to get value for money even though he had $3.3 billion to spend. In the first six months of office Ickes spent only $110 million. Nevertheless, the PWA helped to construct:
- 13000 schools
- 50 miles of road

HAROLD ICKES (1874-1952)

Ickes had been a member of the Republican Party before joining the Democrats. Although he was criticised for using PWA money too slowly, he remained a member of FDR's government until 1945.

WORKS PROGRESS ADMINISTRATION (WPA), APRIL 1935-1943

This agency was created by the Emergency Relief Appropriation Act. It was the most important agency created during the Second New Deal (1935-1937). This agency was also put under the direction of Harry Hopkins, with a budget of $4.8 billion. By the time of its closure in 1943, it had spent $11 billion and had employed eight million. Not only did it build roads, hospitals, schools and airports, it also set up:
- Federal Project One to help musicians and actors
- Federal Writers' Project to aid writers of books, plays and films
- Theatre Project, which employed 11,000 performers and helped future film stars Orson Welles and John Huston
- National Youth Administration, which helped young students stay on at college and university.

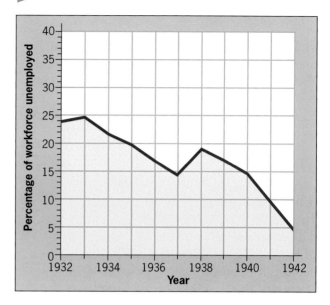

SOURCE 2 — A junior member of FDR's government, talking about the introduction of the CWA in November 1933.

"The government set up the CWA very hurriedly. No means test – any guy could just walk in and get a job. Leaf-raking, cleaning up libraries, painting the town hall – within 60 days, four million were put to work."

Questions

1. Describe the measures taken during the New Deal to reduce unemployment.
2. Study Source 2.
   a) Which of the jobs mentioned do you think were boondoggle jobs?
   b) How useful is this source as evidence of the success of the CWA?
3. In what ways did the work of the FERA differ from the work of the CWA in helping the unemployed?
4. Which New Deal agency do you think did most to help the unemployed? Give reasons for your answer.

The New Deal, finance and industry

FDR did not only want to bring relief to the unemployed. He also wanted to reform the American economy so an economic depression couldn't happen again. Many in America blamed the government's laissez-faire approach to the economy.

FINANCE

The Glass-Steagall Banking Act, June 1933

This act attempted to prevent the kind of bank collapse that occurred during the economic depression after October 1929. It created the Federal Deposit Insurance Corporation (FDIC). This agency guaranteed all bank deposits up to $5000, giving people confidence that their savings in banks would be safe.

Commercial banks existed in every town and city. These were the banks where ordinary Americans put their savings. The act prevented these banks from taking part in stock market share speculation. Such speculation had been an important cause of the Wall Street Crash of October 1929 (see p38).

Between 1933 and 1935, the number of bank closures began to decline rapidly. In 1936, for the first time in 60 years, no national banks collapsed.

Reforming Share Purchases

In May 1933 the Truth in Securities Act was passed. This act aimed to prevent share speculation in stock exchanges by ensuring that all new share purchases were registered with the Federal Trade Commission. In June 1934 the Securities Exchange Act set up the Securities and Exchange Commission (SEC). This agency regulated all stock exchanges across the country.

INDUSTRY

The National Recovery Administration, 1933-1935

The most well-known alphabet agency of the First New Deal was the NRA – the National Recovery Administration. Its symbol, a blue eagle, became the symbol of the New Deal.

The NRA aimed to improve wages and working conditions. All businesses that displayed the Blue Eagle had to agree to pay a minimum wage of $12 for a 40 hour week. As a result, the NRA laid down codes of behaviour for businesses if they wished to obtain the NRA Blue Eagle logo. US citizens were encouraged to buy goods only when they saw the Blue Eagle sign displayed. In all, 750 different NRA codes were created. In trying to regulate trade practices, the NRA attempted to encourage fair competition. As a result, companies were prevented from advertising or price-cutting to gain more sales. New York city's biggest department store, Macy's, was prevented advertising that its goods were sold at six cents below other stores. Henry Ford, whose company made one in four cars in the USA, refused to be involved, declaring, "You ain't sticking blue buzzards on my cars!"

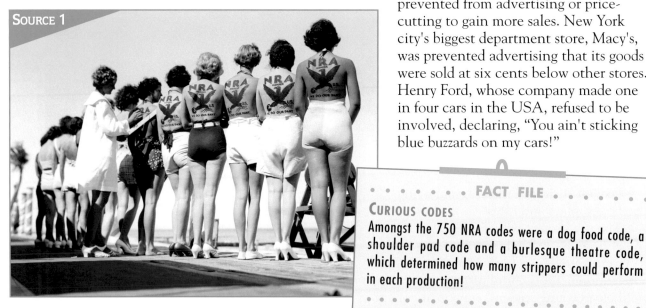

SOURCE 1

Women displaying the NRA Blue Eagle on their backs, September 1933.

FACT FILE

CURIOUS CODES

Amongst the 750 NRA codes were a dog food code, a shoulder pad code and a burlesque theatre code, which determined how many strippers could perform in each production!

GENERAL HUGH JOHNSON (1882-1947)

A former US Army general, Johnson was a controversial head of the NRA. Frances Perkins, the Secretary of Labor, called Johnson "an erratic man, but with strokes genius".

Known for his heavy drinking, Johnson approached the NRA as if it were part of the army. His dictatorial ways earned him many enemies.

SOURCE 2

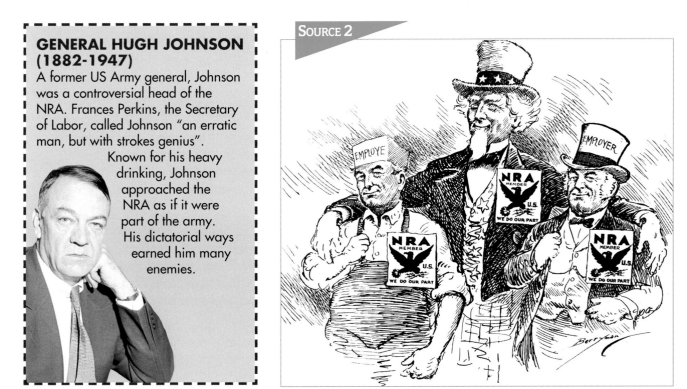

'The Spirit of the New Deal'. This cartoon was produced by the US government in 1933.

INVESTIGATE...

Why was the Blue Eagle chosen as the symbol for the NRA and how popular was the symbol? Visit

www.smithsonianmag.com/smithsonian/issues99/may99/object_may99.html .

SOURCE 3

From one of FDR's radio 'fireside chats' to the American people in 1933.

"Government ought to have the right, and will have the right, to prevent – with the assistance of that industry – all unfair practices, and to enforce that agreement by the authority of government."

Criticism of the NRA

General Hugh Johnson, the head of the NRA, faced considerable opposition to his new regulations. "Hugh, your codes stink!" was the opinion of Harry Hopkins, the head of FERA and CWA. Seven grocers from Cleveland, Ohio, sent a telegram to FDR saying, 'NRA is the worst law ever passed by Congress'. Strikers in Baltimore, Maryland, carried a sign saying, 'NRA means National Run Around'.

Criticism became so great that FDR set up the National Recovery Review Board in March 1934. It heard over 3000 complaints. Eventually, in May 1935, the US Supreme Court declared the NRA unconstitutional and it was discontinued.

Nevertheless, in its short life the NRA did help get many Americans back to work. It spent $3.3 billion on public works to help the unemployed.

unconstitutional
against the US Constitution and therefore illegal

Questions

1. Study Source 1. How does it suggest that the NRA was popular with the American public?
2. Study Source 2.
   a) Describe how the cartoon tries to show that the NRA is important to the USA.
   b) How reliable is this cartoon as evidence of the popularity and importance of the NRA?
3. Study Source 3. How useful is this as evidence of the importance of the NRA to the First New Deal?
4. In what ways did the New Deal try to prevent another Wall Street Crash?
5. Using information and sources in this section, explain how the NRA aimed to outlaw unfair practices in business and industry.

The New Deal and youth

CIVILIAN CONSERVATION CORPS (CCC), MARCH 1933

One of the most popular Alphabet Agencies of the New Deal was the Civilian Conservation Corps (CCC). It was FDR's own idea, and was part of the Unemployed Relief Act passed by Congress on March 31, 1933. The CCC aimed to give work to young, unemployed men. It also hoped to use these young men to improve the land and environment.

To be able to join the CCC, men had to be unmarried, unemployed, and between 18 and 25. The CCC was organised along military lines and was run by a conservative southerner, Robert Fechner. Those involved received one dollar a day pocket money plus a uniform, food and lodging. On top of this, CCC workers earned $30 a month, of which $25 was sent home to their parents.

The young men involved in the CCC worked away from home. They usually lived in tents or wooden huts. Their task was to help improve the countryside (see box, right).

At its height the CCC employed 500,000 young men in 2000 camps across the USA. Eventually the CCC came to an end in 1942, during the early years of the Second World War. In its nine-year existence the CCC enrolled two and a half million men. It helped the young male unemployed to get jobs and taught thousands of them to read and write for the first time. In 1937, in a survey of CCC members, one young man wrote: 'Here they teach you how to pour concrete and lay stones and drive trucks.' However, there was no guarantee of a job once someone had left the CCC.

Also, the membership of the CCC was predominantly white. In states like Mississippi, where African-Americans were a majority, a 1938 survey showed that only 11 per cent of CCC members from that state were black. Equally, the CCC was only limited to men. It took the creation of the Works Progress Administration (WPA) in April 1935 to create similar camps and opportunities for women.

What did the CCC do?

- Prevented soil erosion by planting 220 million trees across the Midwest. This was known as the 'Shelterbelt'. Over 80 per cent of the trees survive today.

- Improved National Parks and set up State Parks across America. For example, Zion National Park, Utah, and Edisto Beach State Park, South Carolina, were built by the CCC.

- Helped extinguish forest fires and, in Wyoming, put out a major fire in a coalmine that had been burning for 70 years.

- Helped to construct reservoirs for irrigation.

- Built six major dams.

- Established programmes to control the breeding of mosquitoes in the South which helped remove the threat of malaria from the USA.

MARY MCLEOD BETHUNE (1875-1955)
Born in South Carolina, McLeod Bethune was one of 17 children. Her parents were former slaves. After a Christian education, she founded the Daytona Institute for Negro Girls and later became president of the National Association of Colored Women. She was Director of Negro Affairs in the NYA from 1936 to 1944. During the Second World War she was an adviser to the US government and, afterwards, to the United Nations.

CCC workers wait for their day's work in Shasta National Forest, California, in 1933.

A CCC poster from 1941.

THE NATIONAL YOUTH ADMINISTRATION (NYA), 1935

The CCC offered immediate work for the unemployed. Most of the work was unskilled, manual labour. However, by the time of the Second New Deal (1935-1937) help was offered to young men and women who wanted a decent education. As part of the Works Progress Administration, a separate National Youth Administration was created in 1935. It provided money for young people to go to university and college.

By the end of 1935 over 200,000 young people were able to stay on at high school in return for doing jobs around their college. By 1937 the NYA was helping young people to get college degrees and become skilled workers such as chefs and mechanics.

Unlike the CCC, the NYA made a big effort to help African-Americans. The NYA had its own Office of Negro Affairs, under the leadership of Mary McLeod Bethune (see p54), an African-American from South Carolina. The Office had its own fund to help young African-Americans gain a college education.

One of the most successful NYA areas was Texas. Here, future president Lyndon B. Johnson helped thousands of students through college and university with state money. He also made a particular effort to get a fair deal for African-American students in a state with a reputation for racial discrimination.

Questions

1. Describe the ways the Civilian Conservation Corps aimed to help young people.
2. In what ways did the CCC differ from the NYA in helping young people during the Depression?
3. Why do you think it was important to help poor and unemployed young people during the Depression years of the 1930s?
4. Which agency, do you think, had a greater impact on the USA during the 1930s: the CCC or the NYA? Give reasons for your answer.

The New Deal and farmers

Even before the start of the Depression in 1929, farmers had faced hardship. Overproduction in the 1920s had led to a drop in prices for farm produce. Once the Depression took hold, the poor position of farmers became even worse. When FDR became President farmers faced:

- Low prices for their produce
- Banks (who owned many farms) reclaiming their land
- A lack of electricity
- Soil erosion and flooding.

So what did FDR do to aid farmers?

AGRICULTURAL ADJUSTMENT ACT, MAY 12 1933

This act created another Alphabet Agency: the Agricultural Adjustment Administration (AAA). It was run by Henry Wallace, Secretary of Agriculture (see biography).

Wallace dealt with the problem of low prices by paying farmers to slaughter livestock and reduce their area of crops. By 1935, 30 million hectares of farmland had been removed from cultivation. By slaughtering livestock, farm supplies fell so that the price for each animal rose.

Many Americans were horrified by the sight of milk being thrown away or livestock slaughtered and buried. These acts were taking place at a time of great economic hardship where many faced the fear of starvation. By 1935 Wallace's actions seemed to have worked. In 1933, farm incomes had been $4.5 billion. Now they were $6.9 billion.

HENRY WALLACE (1888-1965)

Born to a farming family from Iowa, his grandfather had founded a famous farmers' magazine, *Wallace's Farmer*. Wallace had been a member of the Republican Party. However, he resigned in 1928 to join FDR's Democrats. When FDR became President he made Wallace Secretary for Agriculture.

Unfortunately, in 1935, the US Supreme Court declared the Act of 1933 to be unconstitutional and was made illegal. So, in 1938, a second Agricultural Adjustment Act was passed which restored many of the benefits contained in the first act.

FARM CREDIT ADMINISTRATION, 1933

Farmers also faced their farms being repossessed by banks. Farmers usually bought their farms with bank loans. Once the Depression began, many banks closed and others demanded their money back. To prevent further farm closures, FDR set up the Farm Credit Administration that lent money directly to farmers to help them keep their farms.

RESETTLEMENT ADMINISTRATION, 1935

Although the reduction in production and aid with mortgages helped farm owners, it did nothing to help farm workers who did not own farms. The government planned to buy 75 million acres (30 million hectares) in the Midwest and West in which 450,000 farm labourers' families could be resettled. Unfortunately, terrible drought in the West prevented the Resettlement Administration from achieving its targets. Only 5000 families were resettled.

THE DUST BOWL, 1934-1937

A major drought developed in the western states from 1933. It led to the loss of livestock and destroyed the topsoil essential for growing crops. Wind turned the dry topsoil into huge dust storms that turned day into night in many western areas.

Thousands of poor farmers, known as Okies and Arkies (because they came from Oklahoma and Arkansas), fled what became known as 'The Dust Bowl' by going west. Using the highway Route 66, they travelled to southern California in the hope of working in orchards and on farms. Between 1935 and 1940, 350,000 migrated to California from the Dust Bowl area.

Most Okies and Arkies were not welcomed in California. They were forced to live in shanty towns and were paid very low wages. John Steinbeck, the American Nobel Prize-winning novelist, wrote about their fate in *The Grapes of Wrath*, published in 1939.

RURAL ELECTRIFICATION, 1935

co-operative
a group who act together to produce something and share profits from that production

The Rural Electrification Administration (REA) was created to give low interest loans to rural **co-operatives** to provide electricity. In all, 417 co-operatives were created in the late 1930s, providing electricity for over 250,000 by 1939.

TENNESSEE VALLEY AUTHORITY (TVA), 1933 – PRESENT DAY

The longest-lasting Alphabet Agency of the New Deal was the TVA. The TVA attempted to deal with rural poverty in the Upper South, an area with strong support for FDR's Democrat Party. The area's main problems were:

- regular flooding of the Tennessee River
- lack of electricity
- lack of irrigation water
- soil erosion.

During the 1930s the TVA built a network of dams that controlled the flow of the Tennessee River and provided hydroelectric power (see map p49). In 1933 only two per cent of Tennessee Valley farms had electricity. By 1945 this had risen to 75 per cent. Industry was also set up with the creation of a large aluminium-canning factory near the Muscle Shoals dam in Alabama.

Many people criticised FDR for creating the TVA. He was accused of being a socialist because the TVA was government-owned.

FDR replied that the TVA was "Neither fish nor fowl, but it will taste awfully good to the people of the Tennessee Valley."

He was right. The TVA brought major improvements to one of America's formerly undeveloped regions.

SOURCE 1

From a May 1937 copy of *The Readers' Digest*, a nationally produced magazine.

'The Dust Bowl is a dying land. I do not exaggerate when I say that in this country there is now no life for miles and miles; no human beings, no birds, no animals. Only a dull brown land with cracks showing. Hills furrowed with eroded gullies – you have seen pictures like that in ruins of lost civilisations.'

SOURCE 2

Refugees fleeing the Dust Bowl wait for a tyre to be changed, June 1939.

Questions

1. Study Source 1. How useful is it as evidence of the effects of the Dust Bowl on the USA?
2. What were the problems facing farmers in the USA at the start of the New Deal in 1933?
3. In what ways did the AAA and REA help farmers?
4. Which Alphabet Agency do you think brought most help to farmers? Give reasons to support your answer.
5. 'During the New Deal years (1933-1941) all American farmers saw an improvement in their standard of living.' Using all the sources and information in this spread, explain whether or not you agree with this statement.

African-Americans, Native Americans and women

When FDR promised a 'New Deal' for America in 1932, did this promise include African-Americans, Native Americans and Women?

DID THE NEW DEAL HELP AFRICAN-AMERICANS?

The economic depression from 1929 led to very high levels of unemployment amongst African-Americans. By 1931 in the Old South unemployment levels for blacks were over 33 per cent, much higher than for whites. New Deal agencies like the CCC, the TVA and the WPA gave work to African-Americans. However, in the Old South, the system of separating blacks and whites (segregation) continued.

SOURCE 1

A drinking fountain in the Old South during the 1930s.

FDR's wife, Eleanor Roosevelt (see p66), used her influence to aid African-Americans. When the National Youth Administration was created in 1935 it contained a Bureau for Negro Affairs. Eleanor Roosevelt helped persuade FDR to appoint African-American Mary McLeod Bethune to lead it (see p54). The Bureau helped many African-Americans gain a college education.

Perhaps the most important change to help African-Americans came in June 1941, shortly before America's entry into the Second World War. In Presidential Executive Order 8802,

FDR banned racial discrimination in defence industries. This helped tens of thousands of African-Americans gain employment during the war.

WAS LIFE BETTER FOR AFRICAN-AMERICANS BY 1941?

Many blacks had benefited from New Deal programmes. In January 1935, three million African-Americans – 20 per cent of the black labour force – were employed on these programmes. However, they still faced discrimination in jobs, housing and education across America. The situation in the Old South had not changed, and between 1933 and 1935, 63 African-Americans were killed in lynchings (see p17).

Many blacks hoped that FDR would introduce a law banning lynching. However, FDR needed the support of southern white Democrat Senators and Congressmen to pass his New Deal programmes. So nothing was done to stop these terror attacks against southern blacks. Nor was anything done to end segregation in these states. However, in 1938, the US Supreme Court, in a case called *Missouri ex rel Gaines v Canada*, allowed a black student, Lloyd Gaines, to attend the all-white University of Missouri. This was an important case for black civil rights.

Whilst in 1932 more African-Americans voted for Hoover than FDR in the presidential election, from 1936 onwards most African-Americans supported FDR's Democrats.

DID THE NEW DEAL HELP NATIVE AMERICANS?

In 1932 most Native Americans lived on tribal reservations. They were poorly educated and mainly lived in poverty. It was only in 1924 that all Native Americans were given US citizenship.

The Bureau of Indian Affairs dealt with

Native American issues for the Federal Government. In 1934 FDR's Commissioner for Indian Affairs, John Collier, made a number of important changes. In the Indian Reorganisation Act of 1934, Native American culture was safeguarded for the first time. This helped Native Americans maintain their own ways of life. Also, the act reorganised Indian tribes into self-governing bodies. Each tribe was allowed to have its own laws, police and government.

Even though it gave Native Americans more rights, the Act was opposed by 75 of the 245 tribes, including the largest tribe, the Navajo of the South West. By 1941 the economic position of Native Americans had changed little. Most were still desperately poor.

SOURCE 2

An Apache family at San Carlos Indian Reservation, Arizona, in 1939.

HOW DID WOMEN BENEFIT FROM THE NEW DEAL?

In 1933 FDR appointed the first woman to the Cabinet. Frances Perkins (see p64) became Secretary for Labor, a position she occupied throughout the New Deal. However, men still benefited more from the New Deal. This was due in part to the types of job women did. Large numbers of women were in domestic service as cooks, cleaners, or maids. These jobs were not covered by agencies such as the National Recovery Administration (NRA). Even in jobs covered by the NRA, women were given pay rates from 15 per cent to 30 per cent less than men for the same job!

However, in 1935 a Women's and Professional Division was created in the WPA (Works Progress Administration). It helped women get more professional jobs, such as librarians and teachers. Eleanor Roosevelt also set up a conference at the White House on the Emergency Needs of Women to give publicity to the position of women.

SOURCE 3

Adapted from *The New Deal* by historian Tony Badger, 1989. He assesses the role of Eleanor Roosevelt in helping women during the New Deal.

'The success of women in the New Deal years owed much to Mrs Eleanor Roosevelt. She provided a dynamic role model. She also gave women in the New Deal prestige and special access to the President. She was a champion for women's social welfare cause. No **First Lady** had been as independent and as public a figure as Mrs Roosevelt.'

First Lady
the President's wife

Trade unions

The most important development to help women in work was the growth of the trade union movement. The Congress of Industrial Organisations (CIO), a national trade union organisation, encouraged its unions to set up women's groups. By 1940 800,000 women had joined trade unions. They were heavily involved in the textile and clothing industries. The Textile Workers' Union had increased its membership from 20,000 in 1936 to 120,000 by 1943. The Amalgamated Clothing Workers of America (ACWA) had increased its membership from 60,000 in 1932 to 300,000 by 1942. These organisations helped improve pay and working conditions in these industries.

Questions

1. *Study Sources 1 and 2. What do these photographs show about the position of African-Americans and Native Americans in the USA in the 1930s?*
2. *Study Source 3. In what ways did Mrs Eleanor Roosevelt help women and African-Americans during the New Deal?*
3. *'The New Deal did very little to help African-Americans, Native Americans or women.' Do you agree with this statement? Use the sources and information in this section and give reasons for your answer.*

AQA
style

Roosevelt's New Deal

The percentage of
workers unemployed in
the USA, 1924-1939.

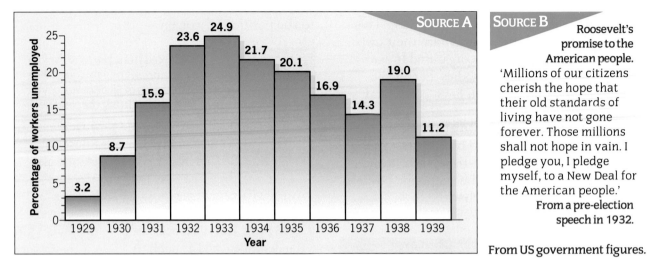

SOURCE A

SOURCE B

Roosevelt's
promise to the
American people.
'Millions of our citizens
cherish the hope that
their old standards of
living have not gone
forever. Those millions
shall not hope in vain. I
pledge you, I pledge
myself, to a New Deal for
the American people.'
From a pre-election
speech in 1932.

From US government figures.

QUESTIONS AND JENNIFER'S ANSWERS

(a) What can we learn from **Source A** about
unemployment in the USA in the 1930s?
(AQA 2003)   *(3 marks)*

> Source A shows the percentage of workers who
> were unemployed in the USA from the start of the
> economic depression to 1939.
>
> You can see that unemployment rose rapidly from
> 1929 to 1933. It rose from 3.2 per cent to 24.9 per cent.
> From this high, unemployment dropped to 14.3 per
> cent in 1937. However, it rose again to 19.0 per cent
> in 1938. This was called the 'Roosevelt Recession'.
> By 1939 unemployment dropped to 11.2 per cent,
> which was still high compared to 1929.

(b) Using **Source A and your own knowledge**, why
was Roosevelt successful in the 1932 presidential
election?
(AQA 2003)   *(7 marks)*

> FDR won the 1932 election because of the
> Depression. Millions of Americans were thrown out
> of work after the Wall Street Crash of 1929. From
> 1929 to 1932 President Hoover had done very little to
> end unemployment. By 1932 hundreds of banks
> had closed and the economy seemed to be
> heading towards a collapse. FDR won the election
> because the unemployed and working people
> voted for him. He gave them hope and he said he
> had a plan to end the Depression. In 1932 most
> states voted for FDR and he won a landslide
> victory.

(c) Describe how Roosevelt dealt with the crisis in
banking in 1933.
(AQA 2003)   *(5 marks)*

> When FDR became President all the banks across
> America were closed. FDR passed the Emergency
> Banking Act. This meant that he would hold a
> four-day banking holiday. In this period he would
> check that all the banks were healthy and in a
> position to conduct business. At the end of the
> period only those banks that were properly run
> were allowed to open. This move gave confidence
> to Americans.

(d) Did the New Deal end the Depression in the USA
in the 1930s? Use **your own knowledge** to
explain your answer.
(AQA 2003)   *(15 marks)*

> The New Deal helped save the USA from
> Depression. When FDR became President 24.9 per
> cent of the US workforce was unemployed. By 1939
> the number had dropped to 11.2 per cent. The New
> Deal did this by creating thousands of jobs
> through Alphabet Agencies. These included the
> CCC, which gave jobs to young men. In 1933-1935
> there was the PWA and the CWA. These gave
> thousands of jobs to people who might otherwise
> have starved. FERA created jobs just to stop people
> from being unemployed. Many were called
> boondoggle jobs because they did little to help
> the economy. Sweeping leaves in parks and

scaring birds off government buildings were some of these jobs.

The New Deal also made many reforms in banking and the economy to prevent another Depression. The Emergency Banking Act and the Glass-Steagall Banking Act, both in 1933, prevented the banking system from collapsing. The New Deal also created the Securities and Exchange Commission to stop share speculation.

Finally, the New Deal helped farmers and specific regions. The AAA gave farmers better incomes. The TVA created electricity in the Tennessee River Valley. It also helped stop soil erosion.

So the New Deal did a lot to help end the Depression. As FDR said, it brought Relief, Recovery and Reform.

HOW TO SCORE FULL MARKS – WHAT THE EXAMINERS SAY

Question (a)
This question requires candidates to understand information contained in a graph.

Jennifer has written a very good answer. She mentions the trends in unemployment from 1929. She refers specifically to the individual years and the exact percentage of unemployment. She also refers to the 'Roosevelt Recession' of 1937-8. Finally, she pointed out that in 1939 unemployment was still higher than in 1929.

As a result, Jennifer received full marks, 3 out of 3.

Question (b)
This question requires candidates to use the information in Source B and their own knowledge

Jennifer uses her own knowledge to answer the question but neglects to use the information in Source B. She does refer to the idea that FDR promised hope to the poor and unemployed, but, by referring to Source B, she could have mentioned that FDR promised a New Deal for the American people as a whole. Had Jennifer organised her answer into separate paragraphs for each point she mentioned, she would have scored higher. She should also have prioritised the various reasons for FDR's success by stating what the most important reason for FDR's election victory was, and explaining how important all the other factors were. Finally, Jennifer should have tried to link the various reasons she gave. For example, the loss of hope under Hoover contrasts with the hope FDR gave America with his promise of a New Deal.

If she had included all these points in her answer she would have gained full marks. Instead she received 3 out of a possible 7 marks.

Question (c)
This question requires candidates to describe the key actions taken by FDR in banking in 1933.

Jennifer deals effectively with the Emergency Banking Act. However, she doesn't mention the Glass-Steagall Banking Act of 1933. This act prevented commercial banks from investing on the stock market. Commercial banks dealt with ordinary American citizens. This change aimed to prevent the type of share speculation which had caused the Wall Street Crash of 1929.

If Jennifer had mentioned all these points she would have received full marks. Her response received 3 out of a possible 5 marks.

Question (d)
This question requires candidates to use their own knowledge to test a view on the success of the New Deal.

Jennifer makes several useful points. Using information in Source A, she mentions the drop in unemployment. She also identifies a number of important areas where the New Deal helped get the USA out of Depression. She mentions several important Alphabet Agencies. She also mentions the way the New Deal helped stabilise the banking system. Unfortunately, her answer is slightly one-sided. Although unemployment dropped to 11.2 per cent of the workforce by 1939, unemployment was still above the 3.2 per cent of 1929. This suggests that the New Deal did not end the Depression. It just made it less severe. She also misses some important agencies such as the WPA. From 1935 until 1942 this was the most important Alphabet Agency in providing help for the unemployed.

As a result, Jennifer received 11 out of a possible 15 marks. To gain higher marks, she needed to produce a more balanced answer.

EXTENSION WORK

Which do you think was the most effective Alphabet Agency of the First New Deal? Explain your answer, **using sources and information from the last chapter and your own knowledge**. *(15 marks)*

• AQA accepts no responsibility whatsoever for the accuracy or method of working in the answers given.

The Second New Deal and labour

HOW DID THE SECOND NEW DEAL DIFFER FROM THE FIRST NEW DEAL?

The First New Deal lasted from March 1933 to January 1935. The Second New Deal began in November 1934, following the mid-term Congress election. The election produced an even bigger majority for the Democrat Party in both the Senate and House of Representatives than the 1932 elections. Many new Party members wanted to pass more reforms to help the poor, the unemployed and working people. Equally, FDR wanted to pass more reform to prevent people supporting more radical critics of the New Deal (see p70). As a result, between 1935 and 1937, the Federal Government and Congress helped pass important Acts which were to change American society. While the First New Deal aimed to stop complete economic collapse, the Second New Deal aimed to reform America.

WHAT PROBLEMS DID TRADE UNIONS FACE?

Trade unions were an increasingly important section of US society. They were groups of working men in industry, who formed organisations to help improve wages and working conditions. They were opposed by big businesses like the Ford Motor Company, which considered them a threat to the smooth running of their businesses. The main American trade union at the beginning of the New Deal was the American Federation of Labor (AFL). This organisation represented skilled workers. Many semi-skilled and unskilled workers were not in a trade union.

semi-skilled
workers who had some training but were not fully qualified

Trade unions also faced problems linked to the Depression. By 1933, 12.8 million workers were unemployed. This made it difficult for trade unions to bargain for better wages.

WHY WAS THE WAGNER ACT OF 1935 IMPORTANT?

One of the most important Acts passed in the Second New Deal was the National Labor Relations Act of July 1935. It was better known as the Wagner Act after Robert Wagner, the Democrat Senator of New York State who was the major force behind it.

The Wagner Act gave trade unions the right to **collective bargaining**. It also allowed workers to join a trade union of their own choice by secret voting, and created a National Labor Relations Board. This board made sure that both employers and trade unions acted correctly.

collective bargaining
the right of a trade union to bargain for the wages of all its members

The Wagner Act helped trade unions to grow, and many semi-skilled and unskilled workers joined trade unions. In November 1935 a new national trade union organisation was formed. This was the Congress of Industrial Organisations (CIO), which was led by the miners' leader, Al Lewis. It represented semi-skilled and unskilled workers such as coalminers and car workers.

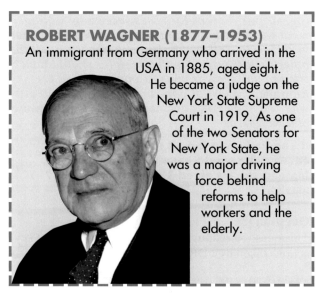

ROBERT WAGNER (1877–1953)
An immigrant from Germany who arrived in the USA in 1885, aged eight. He became a judge on the New York State Supreme Court in 1919. As one of the two Senators for New York State, he was a major driving force behind reforms to help workers and the elderly.

SOURCE 1	The growth of trade unions			
	1930	1932	1934	1940
Total workforce (millions)	50	51	53	56
Total trade union membership (millions)	3.6	3.2	3.2	8.9
Percentage of workforce in trade unions	6.8%	6%	5.7%	15.5%

From a popular trade union song during the New Deal years, called 'Solidarity Forever!'

'What force on earth is weaker
Than the feeble strength of one?
For the union makes us strong.
Solidarity forever
Solidarity forever
For the union makes us strong.'

Motors factory in Flint, Michigan, a 'sit down' strike took place. The workers occupied the factory to stop all production. The Governor of Michigan, Frank Murphy, sent in 1400 **National Guardsmen** to stop the violence between strikers and the General Motors goon squads. After more than a month of the sit-in, General Motors agreed to the strikers' demands. The USA was affected by violent strikes right up to its entry into the Second World War in December 1941.

National Guardsmen
part time soldiers equivalent to Britain's Territorial Army

HOW SUCCESSFUL WAS THE SECOND NEW DEAL IN DEALING WITH LABOUR DISPUTES?

The Wagner Act gave trade unions many rights. Also, in the Second New Deal, the Guffey-Snyder Coal Act of 1935 set minimum prices for coal and a minimum standard of working conditions for coalminers. However, even though trade union membership grew, labour disputes still occurred. A major reason for these disputes was the 'Roosevelt Recession' of 1937–38. FDR's government cut back on public spending in 1937 and this led to a rise in unemployment. It rose from 16.9 per cent of the workforce in 1936 to 19 per cent of the workforce in 1938.

recession
a period when production and prices fall and unemployment increases

Large numbers of industrial disputes took place. These involved strikes for more pay, or against layoffs. As a result, armed groups hired by employers and known as 'goon squads', were used to break up strikes.

In 1937, a new tactic was used by workers to get better pay and conditions. At the General

Food for General Motors strikers in New York is loaded onto a truck. It was provided by a trade union belonging to the CIO.

Questions

1. Study Source 1.
   a) Why do you think trade union membership fell between 1930 and 1934?
   b) Does it support the view that the Wagner Act of 1935 helped the growth of trade union membership? Explain your answer.
2. Study Source 2. What reasons does it give for joining a trade union?
3. Study Source 3. How useful is it as evidence of strikers and trade unions during the Second New Deal? Explain your answer.
4. What changes took place during the Second New Deal that helped trade unions?
5. Do you think the New Deal brought an end to the problems faced by industrial workers? Give reasons for your answer.

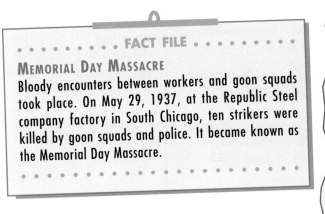

. . . . **FACT FILE** . . . .

MEMORIAL DAY MASSACRE
Bloody encounters between workers and goon squads took place. On May 29, 1937, at the Republic Steel company factory in South Chicago, ten strikers were killed by goon squads and police. It became known as the Memorial Day Massacre.

A LANDMARK REFORM

The USA is a federal country. This means that political power is divided between the central or federal government and state governments. An important part of state government responsibility was to provide help for the poor and needy. In 1935 only 27 of the 48 states provided pensions for the elderly. Only one state, Wisconsin, provided unemployment benefit. This had only been introduced in 1932!

However, in the US Constitution of 1787, it was written that the federal government was expected 'to promote the general welfare' of the American people. FDR used this to pass one of the most important and long lasting parts of the New Deal. This was the Social Security Act of 1935. The main supporters of the Act in FDR's government were Frances Perkins (see biography), the Secretary of Labor, and Harry Hopkins, head of the Works Progress Administration. Unlike virtually every other major industrial country, the USA had no national support for the unemployed and elderly. The Social Security Act changed all that. The money to pay for pensions and

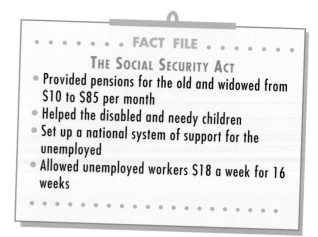

> · · · · · · · FACT FILE · · · · · · · ·
> ## THE SOCIAL SECURITY ACT
> - Provided pensions for the old and widowed from $10 to $85 per month
> - Helped the disabled and needy children
> - Set up a national system of support for the unemployed
> - Allowed unemployed workers $18 a week for 16 weeks
> ·

WHAT CHANGES DID THE SOCIAL SECURITY ACT MAKE?

unemployment benefit came from employers and workers. This was through a three per cent tax on both employers and workers, known as a 'payroll tax'. To complicate matters, the federal government administered the pension scheme while the states *and* the federal government ran the scheme for the unemployed. Pensions were paid on retirement from work at 65 years old. As a result of the Act, every worker in the USA was given a Social Security Number, a system still in use today. Help was given to the blind or disabled, as well as poor or large families.

Yet this did not mean all those in need received the same amount of money. State governments administered the system so that their citizens received different sums of money. A poor child in Massachusetts, New England received $61 a month, while a similar child in Mississippi received only $9 a month.

FRANCES PERKINS (1882-1956)
The first woman to be a Cabinet Minister in US History. Born in New England, she gained a Master of Arts Degree from Columbia University in New York City. In her early career she was a social worker in Massachusetts. When FDR became Governor of New York State he appointed her as Industrial Commissioner, a post she held from 1929 to 1933. She was Secretary of Labor from 1933 to 1945

HOW IMPORTANT WERE THE CHANGES MADE BY THE SOCIAL SECURITY ACT?

The pensions provided by the Act fell far short of the proposals put forward by Dr Francis Townsend in his 'Old Age Revolving Pension Plan' (see p70). Townsend wanted all Americans to receive a pension at 60 years of age. The pension he suggested was $200 a month, not the $85 dollars provided for in the Social Security Act. Even when the Act was passed, groups of Townsend's supporters across the country still pushed FDR's government to increase the amount available.

Not all workers could receive a pension. Agricultural workers and those in domestic service did not receive pensions. The government felt these groups would not be able to pay the contributions needed to get a pension. Yet these workers were the most poorly paid in the country. So, of the 13 million workers in the USA in 1935 in need of a pension, only 550,000 were eligible for one.

SOURCE 1

An American cartoon of 1936. It shows FDR with 'Uncle Sam'.

SOURCE 2

From a British textbook on US history, written in 2000.

'The Social Security Act was possibly the most important and most radical of all the New Deal laws.'

SOURCE 3

Adapted from *New Deal Thought*, by American historian Howard Zinn, 1966. Zinn criticised the New Deal for not going far enough to help those in need.

'The Social Security Act did just enough to help the lowest classes. The Act fell far short of what many in America wanted to see.'

Even though the Act was passed in August 1935, the first pensions were not paid until 1940, from a new Alphabet Agency, the Social Security Administration. Although the unemployed received help for 16 weeks, there was no government support when workers fell ill. The lack of government health insurance still made the USA very different from countries like Britain and France. To this day the USA does not have a national health service. In 1938 the Fair Labor Standards Act established a minimum wage that also helped poorly paid workers.

Questions

1. Study Sources 1 and 2.
   a) In what ways do the two sources have a similar view of the introduction of old age pensions?
   b) How useful is Source 2 as evidence of the importance of the introduction of old age pensions during the Second New Deal?
2. Study Sources 2 and 3. These two sources put forward different interpretations of the importance of the Social Security Act of 1935.
   a) Why do you think they differ in their views?
   b) Which view do you agree with? Explain your answer using information from this section.

Working for the WPA – a case study

THE WORKS PROGRESS ADMINISTRATION (WPA)

When FDR became President in 1933, he promised to bring Relief, Recovery and Reform to America. An important part of this aim was to help the unemployed. In the First New Deal FDR introduced a number of emergency measures to aid those out of work and in need of help. The Federal Emergency Relief Administration (FERA) and the Public Works Administration (PWA) were important parts of the First New Deal. In the winter of 1933 another Alphabet Agency, the Civil Works Administration (CWA), was set up to help the unemployed. However, the most important Alphabet Agency to help the unemployed was created in 1935. This was the Works Progress Administration (WPA), later renamed the Works Projects Administration.

WHY WAS THE WPA SO IMPORTANT?

Helping the unemployed

The WPA was set up under the Emergency Relief Appropriation Act in April 1935. In charge was Harry Hopkins, who had run the FERA and the CWA.

To help the unemployed, the WPA received $4.8 billion from Congress. This was the largest sum of money given to any New Deal agency. The WPA lasted from 1935 to 1943, the middle of the Second World War. In its lifetime the WPA spent $11 billion. At its peak in 1936-1937, the WPA employed three million workers every month. This was about one third of those unemployed in America at the time.

In 1937 FDR cut back on the money available to the WPA. This led to a rise in unemployment and a downturn in economic growth. This period was known as the 'Roosevelt Recession' (see p63). By late 1938 the sum of money given to the WPA rose again, which helped end this period of rising unemployment.

To many, the work offered by the WPA was low paid and very basic. It included simple labouring jobs. However, this was much better than being unemployed and relying on handouts and charity.

SOURCE 1

A WPA work program in Kentucky in 1937. Sandbags are being unloaded from a lorry during a flood.

. . . **FACT FILE** . . .

FROM **1935** TO **1943**, THE **WPA** BUILT:
- 2,500 hospitals
- 5,900 schools
- 350 airports
- 8,000 parks
- 570,000 miles of road

ELEANOR ROOSEVELT (1884-1962)

The wife of President F D Roosevelt was also Theodore Roosevelt's niece and FDR's cousin! Throughout her adult life she supported reform movements. These included the campaign for Votes for Women, helping the poor and needy, and helping improve the position of African-Americans. Throughout the New Deal she was an important adviser to FDR. Despite having six children during their marriage, they were not close. When FDR was Assistant Secretary to the Navy during the First World War he had an affair. After the affair he and Eleanor led almost separate social lives.

HELPING THE ARTS

One of the most important parts of the WPA was its work in helping artists, actors and writers.

- Federal Project One gave work to musicians and actors.
- The Federal Writers' Project was particularly important for African-Americans, who were given government support to help their careers as authors or journalists.
- The Federal Music Project helped fund 38 symphony orchestras across the country.
- Artists were also employed to provide murals and paintings in Federal buildings.
- The Federal Theatre Project employed over 11,000 actors. Rising actors and directors received WPA money to start their careers. These included Orson Welles, who went on to direct some of Hollywood's greatest films, such as *Citizen Kane*, in 1941, and *The Magnificent Ambersons*, in 1944.

SOURCE 4

A WPA artist paints a mural.

SOURCE 2

A WPA poster.

WORK PROMOTES CONFIDENCE

WORKS PROGRESS ADMINISTRATION

SOURCE 3

Adapted from *Anxious Decades*, by American historian Michael Parrish, written in 1992.

'The WPA's bridges, roads and parks made a permanent addition to the nation's wealth. In giving public money to the arts, the WPA laid the foundation for more ambitious federal programs in the 1960s and 1970s, including the National Endowment for the Arts.'

HELPING YOUTH

The National Youth Administration (NYA) was also created by WPA money. It aimed to encourage young people to get work and to stay on in education. Thousands of young Americans from poor families were able to get a university education for the first time.

The NYA also included a section for African-Americans. This was the Bureau of Negro Affairs. It was led by African-American, Mary McLeod Bethune. She was helped in her appointment by the President's wife, Eleanor Roosevelt.

Questions

1. Study Source 1. 'The work shown here is basic and therefore of little value.'
   Do you agree or disagree with this view? Explain your answer.
2. Study Source 2.
   a) What statement is the poster trying to make about the WPA?
   b) How useful is this poster to an historian writing about the WPA?
3. Study Source 3 and use information from this section. Do you agree or disagree with the Michael Parrish's views about the WPA? Explain your answer.
4. Study Source 4. What evidence does the photograph provide about the type of work offered by the WPA to artists?

Poland to Pearl Harbor – the USA goes to war

HOW DID THE SECOND WORLD WAR IN EUROPE AFFECT THE USA?

On September 3, 1939, the Second World War began. In response to Hitler's invasion of Poland, Britain and France declared war on Germany. The USA did not enter the war in 1939. It took the Japanese attack on the US naval base at Pearl Harbor in the Hawaiian Islands (December 7, 1941) to be forced into fighting.

WHY DID FDR STAY OUT OF EUROPEAN AFFAIRS BEFORE SEPTEMBER 1939?

FDR was very concerned about the rise of dictatorships in Europe during the 1930s. In particular he feared the rise of Nazi Germany. However, there was little he could do before 1939. Britain and France had followed a policy of appeasement towards Hitler until April 1939. FDR realised there was little the USA could do without British and French support.

> **appeasement**
> *a policy followed by Britain and France that aimed to avoid war by giving territory to Germany and Italy*

Also Congress had passed two Neutrality Acts in 1935 and 1937 (see p21) that made sure the USA would not become involved in European War. These Acts stated that the USA could not trade with a country at war or give that country financial assistance.

HOW MUCH DID THE USA AID BRITAIN FROM 1939 TO DECEMBER 1941?

The Cash and Carry Plan
In November 1939 FDR was able to persuade Congress to pass the Cash and Carry Plan. This plan changed the Neutrality Acts. Now Britain and France could buy US military equipment as long as they transported it across the Atlantic Ocean in their own ships.

The Plan did little to help France. By June 1940 the German Army had completely defeated France. From 1940 to 1944 France was under German control. From June 1940 Britain was left to stand alone against Germany and its allies like Italy.

However, in September 1940 the USA gave Britain 50 First World War destroyers in exchange for US bases on British controlled islands in the West Indies.

Lend Lease
In March 1941 FDR brought more aid to Britain. The Lend Lease scheme, was introduced. Under the scheme, the USA loaned Britain military equipment and food until the end of the war. Without this aid, Britain would not have been able to continue its war with Germany.

The Atlantic Charter
In August 1941 FDR held a secret meeting with British Prime Minister, Winston Churchill, at Placentia Bay in Newfoundland, Canada. At that meeting both leaders signed the Atlantic Charter. Although the USA had yet to enter the war, this agreement suggested that Britain and the USA would work together against dictators like Hitler.

> **SOURCE 1**
>
> - Both FDR and Churchill agreed to oppose territorial expansion if it was against the wishes of the people concerned.
> - FDR agreed that US naval forces should escort convoys from the USA as far as mid-Atlantic.
> - FDR and Churchill agreed that, after the war, states that had invaded other states should be disarmed.
> - FDR and Churchill agreed to set up a new world system to keep peace.

The main points of the Atlantic Charter, August 15, 1941.

WHY DID IT TAKE THE USA SO LONG TO ENTER THE SECOND WORLD WAR?

Opposition and elections
Even though FDR and his government supported Britain against Germany, many Americans were opposed to going to war. The famous aviator Charles Lindbergh helped lead

the 'America First Committee' which wanted to keep the USA out of a European war. Moreover, FDR wanted to be re-elected president for an unprecedented third time in November 1940. In his electoral campaign he won votes by saying he would not force the USA into war.

Preparing for war

Even though the USA stayed out of the war until December 1941, FDR did prepare the USA for war. On September 16, 1940, compulsory military service was introduced for the first time during peacetime.

During 1941 US naval forces escorted convoys across the western Atlantic. On July 7, 1941, US forces occupied Iceland as part of this plan. By December 1941 several sections of the US navy had been attacked by German U-boats (submarines). On September 4, USS Greer was attacked. On October 17, USS Kearny was torpedoed with the loss of 11 lives.

WHY DID THE JAPANESE ATTACK PEARL HARBOR?

Hitler was not the only dictator FDR feared. He also feared Japanese expansion in the Far East. From 1937 Japan had been at war with China and had occupied most of eastern China. In 1940 Japan occupied the French colony of Indo-China (modern day Vietnam). To try to stop Japanese expansion, FDR persuaded Congress to ban all exports of oil to Japan. This ban, it was hoped, would force Japan to the conference table and bring an end to her expansion in the Far East. Instead, the Japanese government tried to win a quick war against the USA by destroying its Pacific Fleet at Pearl Harbor. In particular, the Japanese wanted to destroy the American aircraft carrier force. So, on December 7, 1941, the Japanese launched a surprise air attack. They inflicted severe damage to many US battleships and killed 2000 US citizens. Unfortunately for the Japanese, the US carrier force was at sea and untouched by the attack.

On December 8 FDR asked Congress to declare war on Japan. On December 11 Hitler declared war on the USA. Hitler believed the USA had already become involved in the European war by aiding Britain.

SOURCE 2

An American cartoon of 1940.

SOURCE 3 The impact of the war in Europe on the US economy, 1938-1942.

YEAR	Percentage unemployed	Industrial production, with 1926 as base year of 100
1938	19.0%	92
1940	14.6%	132
1942	4.7%	220

Questions

1. Study Source 1. Explain how the Atlantic Charter helped force the USA towards joining Britain in the War against Germany.
2. Study Source 2.
   a) What statement is this cartoon trying to make about US policy in 1940?
   b) How reliable is the cartoon as evidence of US opinion in 1940?
3. Study Source 3.
   a) By what percentage did industrial production rise between 1938 and 1940?
   b) Explain why the European war of 1939 to 1941 helped the US economy to grow.

Opposition to the New Deal

FDR once said, "Everyone is against me except the voters."

This suggests that the New Deal faced a lot of opposition. However, it also suggests that, in spite of this opposition, FDR was popular with the electorate. He is the only President in US history to have won four presidential elections – 1932, 1936, 1940 and 1944. In fact, he died in office in April 1945. So who opposed FDR and the New Deal?

LIBERTY LEAGUERS: OPPOSITION FROM THE RIGHT

The Liberty League was founded in April, 1934. It was supported by businessmen who disliked government interference in the economy. Not only did it attract members of the Republican Party, it also attracted conservative Democrats. These included Al Smith, who had been Democrat Presidential candidate in 1928. They attacked FDR throughout the New Deal years, claiming that he was a socialist.

HUEY P LONG, 'THE KINGFISH'

Huey P Long was a Democratic Senator from the southern state of Louisiana. He criticised the First New Deal (1933-1935) for not doing enough to help the poor. In February 1934 he launched the 'Share Our Wealth' campaign. With his slogan of 'Every man a king', he believed all private fortunes over $3 million should be taken by the government, who would then use the money to guarantee every family $2000 a year.

The Share Our Wealth campaign became very popular and made Long a nationally-known figure. In 1935 many thought he might beat FDR to the Democrat nomination for the 1936 presidency. However, in September 1935, he was assassinated by a former supporter.

FATHER CHARLES COUGHLIN, THE RADIO PRIEST

Father Coughlin was a Roman Catholic priest. He had a radio programme called 'The Golden Hour of the Little Flower'. This programme was very popular and attracted weekly audiences of between 30 to 40 million listeners. In 1933, he had initially supported the New Deal. By 1935, however, he felt FDR was not doing enough to help the poor. He wanted the government to take over the banking system. Through his organisation the 'National Union for Social Justice' he formed an alliance with Long's

supporters and the supporters of Francis Townsend. In the 1936 presidential election they formed the Union Party and put up William Lemke as candidate. He received 892,000 votes compared to FDR's 27.7 million!

Father Charles Coughlin

Huey P Long

FRANCIS TOWNSEND AND PENSIONS

Townsend was a retired doctor who supported the idea of old age pensions for all Americans. Up to 1935 the USA had no government-financed pension scheme. He suggested that all people out of work and over 60 should receive $200 a month. Not only would this increase their wealth, it would also increase spending and, with it, the production of goods. Although Townsend's scheme would have been very expensive to fund, it was popular. In 1935 he had five million supporters in pro-Townsend 'Clubs' across America. However, his movement collapsed in 1936 when his business partner was caught stealing funds. Nevertheless, it did encourage FDR to introduce pensions in the Second New Deal (1935-1937).

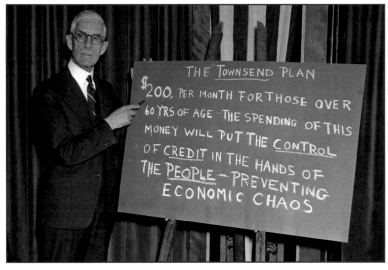

Francis Townsend demonstrates his plan for pensions.

COMMUNISTS AND SOCIALISTS

These groups criticised the New Deal because they believed FDR was trying to save the US economic system – a system they regarded as unfair and prone to depression. They wanted the government to end all private ownership of businesses and factories. This meant the government would take over running the economy. The communists wanted the USA to model itself on the economic changes made by Stalin in the USSR.

At the height of their popularity, the communists and socialists made little impact on American politics. In the 1936 presidential election the Socialist candidate, Norman Thomas, gained 187,000 votes and the Communist, Earl Browder, just 79,000.

UPTON SINCLAIR

In California, the novelist Upton Sinclair put forward the idea that the unemployed should be given work by government-owned co-operatives. They would receive a form of payment that could only be spent in other co-operatives. This idea formed the basis of the 'End Poverty in California' campaign, which aimed to bring social security to the poor and unemployed. Sinclair ran for the office of Governor of California in 1934, but failed to win.

SOURCE 1

From *The New Deal*, by Professor Tony Badger, 1989

'Coughlin, Townsend and Long had much in common. They all came to hate Roosevelt bitterly and they all addressed real problems and real New Deal failings: the insufficiency of economic recovery, the plight of the old and the uneven distribution of wealth. But the solutions they offered were not a serious challenge to the New Deal. They offered simple solutions that could not be put into effect without the creation of a massive state apparatus.'

Questions

1. Study Source 1.
   a) According to the source, why was the opposition of Coughlin, Townsend and Long never a real challenge to FDR's New Deal?
   b) How useful is this source as evidence of opposition to FDR during the New Deal?
2. Why did Coughlin, Townsend and Long criticise the New Deal?
3. How did the criticisms of the Liberty League differ from the criticisms of communists and socialists?
4. "Everyone is against me except the voters". In what ways do you agree or disagree with this view of the amount of opposition to the New Deal during the 1930s?

The New Deal and the US Supreme Court

The most serious opposition to the New Deal did not come from the Republican Party, the Liberty League or left wing politicians. It came from nine elderly men: the justices on the US Supreme Court. This court, along with the President and Congress, made up the federal government (see p9). The US Supreme Court had immense power. It could interpret the meaning of the US Constitution. This allowed it to declare acts by the President, Congress or states unconstitutional and therefore illegal. Its decisions were almost impossible to change. The nine justices were nominated by Presidents

but had to be approved by the Senate. Once appointed, they were in office for life although, like the President, they could be impeached. The only way a Supreme Court decision could be changed was by amending the Constitution. Since 1787 only 29 amendments have been made and ten of these were made in 1791!

FACT FILE

PRESIDENTS FACING IMPEACHMENT

Since 1787 only three Presidents have faced impeachment: Andrew Johnson (1868), Richard Nixon (1974), and Bill Clinton (1999). None were impeached. Although it looked likely that Nixon would be, he resigned beforehand.

THE SCHECHTER 'SICK CHICKEN' CASE, MAY 1935

The Schechter Brothers were a firm based in New York City. They were accused of selling diseased chickens. As a result they were prosecuted by the National Recovery Administration (NRA) for breaking one of its codes about selling goods (see p52).

The Schechter Brothers decided to challenge the prosecution by taking their case to the Supreme Court.

The Chief Justice of the Supreme Court in 1935 was Charles Evan Hughes, a former Republican presidential candidate. Under his leadership, the court declared that the federal government had exceeded its power by setting up the NRA. The federal government could regulate trade and commerce between states, but it could not regulate commerce within states. As the Schechter Brothers planned to sell their diseased chickens within New York State, the federal government had no right to prosecute them.

As a result, the NRA was declared unconstitutional and had to be disbanded.

The Supreme Court attacks the New Deal

In January 1936 the Supreme Court declared the Agricultural Adjustment Administration (AAA) unconstitutional. Again, the Court accused FDR's government of exceeding its powers.

In all, the US Supreme Court declared 11 New Deal laws unconstitutional. Considering that, from 1789 to 1933, the Supreme Court had opposed only 50 federal Acts, it shows how serious the Court's attack on the New Deal was.

These Supreme Court decisions overturned the policies of FDR and the Congress. Virtually on its own, the Court had the power to destroy the whole New Deal.

THE COURT PACKING CRISIS OF 1937

In November 1936 FDR won a landslide victory in the presidential elections, winning in 46 of the 48 states. His Democrat Party also did well in elections to the House of Representatives and the Senate.

However, despite all this political support, FDR still had to face the Supreme Court. He feared that the major reforms of the Second New Deal (1935-1937) would be declared unconstitutional as well. These reforms included old age pensions, social security and the WPA. FDR saw a way around this problem.

In February 1937 he sent the Judicial Procedures Reform Bill to Congress for approval. In 1937 six of the nine Supreme Court justices were over 70 years old. FDR's Bill stated that no justice could serve beyond the age of 70. The Bill also planned to increase the size of the court from nine to 15. If passed, this Bill would give FDR immense power. He would be able to nominate 12 justices, all favourable to him. This would effectively end the Supreme Court's opposition.

Even with FDR's considerable popularity, many thought he had gone too far with his Court 'packing' plan. FDR was accused of trying to become a dictator. By 1937 most of Europe had fallen under dictatorship and some feared the USA might follow.

FDR's plan fails

FDR's plan to reform the Supreme Court was undermined when the Court decided to accept his Social Security Act as legal on May 24. This became known as 'the switch in time that saved nine'. Because it was an Act in favour of FDR, it seemed to eradicate the need to reform the Court. The nine justices retained their seats. Even more in FDR's favour was the retirement that year of justice Willis van Devanter, which allowed FDR to appoint his own nominee, Hugo Black. The dangerous political situation had been defused.

As a result of these changes, the Second New Deal did not suffer in the way the NRA and AAA had. By 1938, the Supreme Court no longer declared New Deal Acts unconstitutional.

Unfortunately for FDR, his reputation and popularity never fully recovered. Although he continued until 1945, the New Deal had reached its highpoint by 1936.

SOURCE 1 Two US cartoons presenting different views on FDR and the Supreme Court.

THE ILLEGAL ACT.
PRESIDENT ROOSEVELT. "I'M SORRY, BUT THE SUPREME COURT SAYS I MUST CHUCK YOU BACK AGAIN."

SOURCE 3 Adapted from *FDR and the New Deal*, by William Leuchtenburg, 1963.

'In attempting to alter the Court, Roosevelt had attacked one of the symbols which many believed the nation needed for its sense of unity. The greater the insecurity of the times, the more people clung to the few institutions which seemed changeless. When Senator Bailey announced his opposition to the plan, a South Carolina lady wrote, 'Bully for you. Don't, don't let that wild man in the White House do this dreadful thing to our country.'

Questions

1. Study Source 1.
   a) Describe what is taking place in both cartoons.
   b) Explain how these two cartoons differ in their views on the problems FDR faced with the Supreme Court.
2. Study Source 2. According to this, why did ordinary Americans dislike FDR's Court packing plan of 1937?
3. Explain why the US Supreme Court was able to declare parts of the First New Deal illegal.

The New Deal – success or failure?

DID THE NEW DEAL END ECONOMIC DEPRESSION?

FDR won the 1932 presidential election on the promise of offering the American people a 'New Deal'. This suggested that he would end the economic depression. In this aim FDR was only partially successful.

Study the information contained in Source 1. You will see that during the New Deal unemployment fell steadily from its high point in 1933 up until 1937. This can be attributed to New Deal programmes to help the unemployed, like the PWA, CWA, TVA, and CCC. However, unemployment rose again from 1937 to 1939 during the period known as the 'Roosevelt Recession'. It was caused by a cut in federal government spending on programmes to help the unemployed.

It was only after 1939 that unemployment really dropped quickly. This was due to the outbreak of the Second World War in Europe. Initially, the war led to an increase in demand for American weapons by Britain and France. The increased demand for weapons meant more munitions factories were built and more people were put to work in them. Then, once the USA entered the war at the end of 1941, unemployment dropped rapidly. Millions of Americans joined the armed forces and more were working for the war effort at home.

FDR stated that, "Dr New Deal stopped the patient [the US economy] from dying. Dr Second World War brought about a complete recovery".

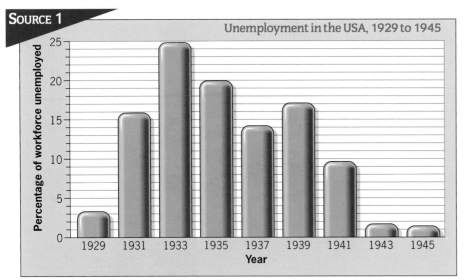

Unemployment in the USA, 1929 to 1945

Two US cartoons of 1936. They provide different views of the New Deal.

A

B

Relief, Recovery and Reform?

FDR had promised the American people 'Relief, Recovery and Reform'. He was successful in bringing relief for the unemployed, but he was only partly successful in bringing about economic recovery before 1942.

The New Deal faced many critics. Some, like Huey P Long, believed FDR was not radical enough in his plans to end the Depression. In fact, FDR had no plan at all. Instead, he created a large number of Alphabet Agencies, which were costly to run.

DID THE NEW DEAL CHANGE AMERICAN GOVERNMENT AND POLITICS?

In 1932 the only member of the federal government that most Americans met regularly was the postman. By 1941 the role of the federal government had grown rapidly. Agencies such as the WPA and CCC offered work to thousands. The federal government also organised social security, like pensions.

To deal with the growth of government, Washington DC developed into a major city. The job of the President also grew. In 1939 FDR created the Executive Office of the President to help him run the country.

> **SOURCE 3**
> From *New Deal Thought*, by Howard Zinn, 1966. Zinn was a left wing historian who believed FDR had not done enough to help the poor.
>
> 'What the New Deal did was to help middle class America, to restore jobs to half the jobless, and to give just enough to the lower classes to create goodwill.'

> **SOURCE 4**
> From *Coming of Age*, a history of inter-war America by Donald McCoy, 1973. McCoy takes a more supportive view of FDR and the New Deal.
>
> 'Roosevelt must be credited with achieving much that was accomplished by the New Deal. In its willingness to experiment, his administration was able to test a broad range of responses to the economic depression. Many of those responses proved successful. If New Deal programmes were sometimes foolish, and occasionally administered poorly, that was the price to pay for experimentation and it was a price most Americans were willing to pay.'

In politics, the Democrats replaced the Republicans as the major party. They controlled the government and US Congress for most of the period from 1933 to 1953.

National government also saw the appointment of large numbers of Democrat-supporting Irish, Jewish and Italian Americans for the first time. However, African-Americans, Native Americans and women made only very limited gains during the New Deal years.

AN ASSESSMENT OF FDR AND THE NEW DEAL

In his attempt to end the economic depression, FDR faced a huge task. He had to persuade both houses of Congress to pass laws. He had to work with the 48 states to make sure these laws functioned. From 1933 to 1937 he faced the opposition of the US Supreme Court, which declared many New Deal laws illegal.

In his task FDR possessed one great characteristic: the power to persuade. He persuaded Congress and most states to help make the New Deal a success. Through the use of radio and newsreel at the cinema he persuaded the American people to trust him.

FDR may not have brought economic prosperity back by 1941, but he did prevent economic collapse. He also restored hope in the American government.

Questions

1. Study Source 2.
   a) How does cartoon A (left) suggest that the New Deal was wasteful in the use of taxpayers' money?
   b) Why do you think there were such different views of the New Deal by 1936?
   c) Which cartoon do you think gives the most accurate view of the New Deal? Explain your answer.
2. Study Sources 3 and 4. Explain why these two historians have different interpretations of the success of the New Deal.
3. 'FDR was successful in dealing with America's economic problems.' Explain whether you agree or disagree with this statement. Use the sources and information in this section to explain your answer.

Writing Essays

In all of the major examination boards students will be expected to engage in extended writing – i.e., writing essays. Essay questions usually carry the highest marks on the examination paper. Like source-based questions, essay questions are marked by a 'Levels of Response' mark scheme. **This means that it is the quality of your answer, more than the quantity of material you produce, that is important.** When answering essay-type questions also refer to the Study Skills section at the beginning of this book. The essay question asked here is common to all the examination boards.

QUESTION AND JOSHUA'S ANSWER

Was the New Deal a success or failure? Explain your answer.   *(15 marks)*

- This question requires you to use your own knowledge of the New Deal.

- You will be expected to explain in what ways the New Deal was a success.

- You will also have to show in what ways it was a failure.

- At the start of the essay, you will have to write a brief and to-the-point introduction.

- At the end of the essay, you will have to provide a concluding paragraph containing a **judgement** about whether the New Deal was a success or failure.

- Even before you begin to write your answer, you should plan what you are going to write. This will help you order your factual knowledge in a way that will get you the highest possible marks.

- You should also remember to write your answer in paragraphs. You should provide a paragraph for each separate point you mention.

When FDR became President in 1933 the USA was in a very bad economic depression. Millions were out of work. Roosevelt promised a New Deal for the American people to end the Depression.

In many ways the New Deal was a success. A big problem for America in the Depression was the collapse of banks. In 1933 FDR introduced two laws that helped stop the banking collapse. During his first 100 days in office he passed the Emergency Banking Act. This restored confidence in the banks. Only those banks which had government approval were allowed to open for business. Also in 1933, the Glass-Steagall Banking Act stopped high street banks from taking part in share speculation on the stock exchange. This had caused many banks to close following the Wall Street Crash.

The New Deal also helped the unemployed. FDR created the Public Works Administration in 1933. This gave jobs to those out of work. In the winter of 1933 to 1934 he also set up the Civil Works Administration. This gave emergency help to the unemployed during the winter months. Both these alphabet agencies cut the number of unemployed. In 1935 FDR set up the Works Progress Administration. This poured billions of dollars into helping the unemployed. These agencies all helped get America out of the Depression.

FDR also helped young people. The Civilian Conservation Corps gave jobs to young men. They lived in camps run by the army. They helped plant forests and develop National and State Parks.

In the Tennessee Valley, FDR created the TVA. This Alphabet Agency helped build dams and produce electricity for a poor area of the USA. The damming of the Tennessee River also controlled flooding and soil erosion. This greatly helped the area known as the Upper South.

The New Deal also helped farmers. The Agricultural Adjustment Act of 1933 helped stabilise farm prices. Farmers were paid to destroy crops and animals in order to limit supply. This helped prevent farmers from going bankrupt. However, in the mid 1930s a great 'Dust Bowl' was created in Arkansas and Oklahoma. This was caused by soil erosion. Thousands of farm families were forced to leave their farms. They went to California.

Although the New Deal helped to cut unemployment it did not bring an end to the Depression. Even in 1941, millions were still out of work. In fact, between 1937 and 1938 unemployment rose again for a time. This was known as the 'Roosevelt Recession'.

Also, some of the New Deal agencies were badly organised. The National Recovery Administration tried to create codes of practice for hundreds of industries. These created problems for businesses trying to get out of depression. In 1935 the Supreme Court declared the NRA illegal because it had taken too much power from the states.

The New Deal did little to help African-Americans. Although they got jobs in the PWA and WPA, they were still regarded as second-class citizens. The New Deal also did little to help Native Americans. Most still lived in poverty on Indian Reservations.

The New Deal did have several failures. However, it was quite successful in other ways. It stopped the US economy from complete collapse. Also the American people thought it quite a success: they re-elected FDR in 1936, 1940 and 1944.

HOW TO SCORE FULL MARKS – WHAT THE EXAMINERS SAY

Joshua's answer is clearly structured. He writes a brief, relevant introduction. His answer is also divided into separate paragraphs. Each paragraph deals with a specific area of the New Deal.

He deals with areas of success first and then he covers areas of failure.

In his conclusion he sums up his answer effectively. He mentions that the New Deal was only a partial success. He is also able to provide evidence to show exactly how far it was successful.

Finally, Joshua wrote his answer to a very good standard of spelling, grammar and punctuation.

This final point helped ensure that Joshua received full marks, 15 out of 15.

EXTENSION WORK

'The New Deal achieved its aims'. Explain whether you agree or disagree with this statement, **using sources and information from the last chapter and your own knowledge.**

• Edexcel accepts no responsibility whatsoever for the accuracy or method of working in the answers given.

ACKNOWLEDGEMENTS

Every effort has been made to contact the holders of copyright material, but if any have been inadvertently overlooked the publishers will be pleased to make the necessary arrangements at the first opportunity.

The author and publishers gratefully acknowledge the use of examination questions from the following awarding bodies.

Assessment and Qualifications Alliance 34-5, 60-1; OCR 46-7.

The publishers would like to thank the following for permission to reproduce pictures on these pages.

(T=Top, B=Bottom, L-Left, R=Right, C=Centre)

© Bettmann/Corbis 10T, 14, 17, 18, 22T, 26, 28, 29, 37, 39, 41, 46L, 52, 53L, 56, 57, 58, 63, 64, 66B, 70, 71, © Corbis 31B, 42L, 50, 51, 54, 55, 59, 62, 66T, 67, © Hulton-Deutsch Collection/Corbis 12, © Swim Ink/Corbis 10B, 22B, © Underwood & Underwood/Corbis 31T, © Oscar White/Corbis 42R, 44;
First National/Charles Chaplin, courtesy The Kobal Collection 30R, United Artists, courtesy The Kobal Collection 30L, Warner Brothers, courtesy The Kobal Collection 25; Peter Newark's American Pictures 15, 24, 27, 48, 53R, 74L; Popperfoto 16; © Punch Ltd 73L; United Artists courtesy The Ronald Grant Archive 19.

Cover picture: Portrait of Franklin Delano Roosevelt, c.1930's. Courtesy The Franklin D.Roosevelt Library, USA.

Index